worship

reforming tradition

Thomas J. **talley**

The Pastoral Press

Washington, DC

ISBN: 0-912405-70-8

The Pastoral Press
225 Sheridan Street, NW
Washington, D.C. 20011
(202) 723-1254

The Pastoral Press is the publications division of the National
Association of Pastoral Musicians, a membership organization of
musicians and clergy dedicated to fostering the art of musical
liturgy.

Printed in the United States of America

Contents

ABBREVIATIONS

CSCO = Corpus scriptorum Christianorum orientalium

CSEL = Corpus scriptorum ecclesiasticorum Latinorum

DACL = Dictionnaire d'archéologie chrétienne et de liturgie

PG = Migne, *Patrologia Graeca*

PL = Migne, *Patrologia Latina*

PO = *Patrologia orientalis*

Introduction

IN MAY 1988 I RECEIVED FROM THE PASTORAL PRESS A SUGGESTION THAT I assemble for publication a collection of my essays that have appeared in various places at various times during the quarter century that I have devoted to teaching and writing about the liturgy. That suggestion was profoundly gratifying, and I agreed to it at once, especially since the publisher generously offered to prepare the manuscript from photocopies of the original publications.

I remain deeply grateful for that invitation from the publisher. However, in seeking to assemble the materials, I was confronted immediately with an old neurosis, an unreasonable anxiety over the fact that I have not always known what I know now. While I have found in these essays no major positions that I would now wish to repudiate or abdicate, each of them has required corrections of detail, clarification of expression, and incorporation of some findings of further research. In addition to all that, in many cases it has been necessary to rewrite introductory and concluding passages in order to accomodate to the requirements of such a volume as this essays written for specific settings, and also to supply documentation for some papers not originally intended for publication. Therefore, while there is little that is new here, there is also little that is unrevised, and a few pieces have been rather thoroughly rewritten. Even so, I have not tried to erase all the evidences of development, and behind the revisions the signs of earlier uncertainties are still perceptible, and may turn out to be closer to the truth.

I would like to express my gratitude for permission to reissue the essays presented here to those publications and institutions for which they were orginally written. The first essay, "Priesthood, Baptism and Ordination," began as the opening presidential address at the seventh congress of *Societas Liturgica* at Washington, D.C., in 1979, and was subsequently published as, "Ordination in Today's Thinking," in *Studia Liturgica*, vol. 13, also issued under the title, *Ordination Rites Past and Present*, edited by Wiebe Vos and Geoffrey Wainwright. Chapters 2, 4, and 6 first appeared in *Worship* and are republished here with the permission of the editor, Kevin Seasoltz, O.S.B. Chapter 2 represents a revision of "The Literary Structure of the Eucharistic Prayer," *Worship* 58 (1984). Chapters 4 and 6 appeared under their present titles in *Worship* 46 (1972) and 47 (1973). The latter of those was first presented at the Twenty-fifth Anniversary Institute of Liturgical Studies of Valparaiso University in February, 1973. Chapter 5, "The Liturgy of Reconciliation," is one of the more thoroughly rewritten essays, but it originated as a contribution to a symposium constituting The George Craig Stewart Memorial Lectures for 1984 at Seabury-Western Theological Seminary. In its present form it incorporates a note on the imposition of ashes that first appeared in *The Living Church* for February 22, 1987. Chapter 7 was originally presented to the Liturgy Master Theme at the Eighth International Patristic Conference at Oxford in 1979, and is reissued here with the permission of Pergamon Press, publishers of *Studia Patristica* XVII in which this essay appeared. Chapter 8 first appeared in *Liturgy* 5.2 (Fall, 1985) under the title, "The Evolution of a Feast," and is reissued here with the permission of The Liturgical Conference. Chapter 9 was an address delivered to the annual conference of the Association of Diocesan Liturgical and Music Commissions in 1987 and was published in December of that year in *Open*, the newsletter of Associated Parishes. Chapters 3 and 10 have not been published previously. "The Windsor Statement and the Eucharistic Prayer" was delivered to a symposium on Anglican/Roman Catholic relations jointly organized by The General Theological Seminary and Fordham University in 1983. The final essay began as an extracurricular lecture to the summer graduate program in liturgical studies at Notre Dame University in 1981. The total project of readying these essays for edition has made me once again mindful of the observation of the distinguished former Professor of Ancient History at Columbia University, E.J. Bickerman, who said in the preface to the English edition of his *Chronology of the Ancient World*, "knowledge is required to prepare a work of scholarship, but only ignorance gives the courage to publish it."

As will be seen, this volume does not aim at maintaining an even level of style or of difficulty. Among the papers found here are some that originated in presentations to scholarly audiences of considerable sophistication, and others that were addressed to beginning students of the liturgy. Some have been included because they represent detailed exposition of difficult material, others because they sidestep details in favor of presenting a general overview. If there is one unifying characteristic, it is that each essay attempts to understand its topic through close examination of the historical data of our patterns of worship, and to locate our present practice within the shifting landscape of the tradition. To what extent that attempt has met with success must, of course, be left to the judgement of others. The attempt, in any case, has been made out of the conviction that our present patterns of worship and their continuing reform need to be seen within a continuity, a tradition, that directs our attention beyond unexamined presuppositions and the fashions of the moment, and that calls us to the authenticity and wholeness of the faith once delivered and ever living.

1

Priesthood in Baptism and Ordination

ONE OF THE MORE IMPORTANT DEVELOPMENTS TOWARD ECUMENICAL convergence in this second half of the twentieth century has been the renewed appreciation of the church as a priestly community. This is nothing new, of course, and such New Testament texts as 1 Peter 2:9 and Apocalypse 5:10 were widely cited by the Fathers and in the Reformation. In the Greek and Latin New Testaments we find the classical terms for those who perform sacred rites (the Greek *hiereus*, the Latin *sacerdos*) applied not to the apostles nor to any other distinct ministerial subgroup, but to all the baptized.

The Meaning of "Priest"

Very quickly, however, the sacrificial understanding of the eucharist led to the more specific application of sacerdotal terminology to those who presided over the rite. Bishops, in the first instance, and then the presbyters who concelebrated with them, came to be spoken of as exercising *sacerdotium*. In writings of the sixth century or so, one must carefully examine the context to be sure whether a reference to a *sacerdos* has in mind a bishop or a presbyter, but it almost surely does not refer to the laity. By the eleventh century, it is virtually always the presbyter that is meant when the term *sacerdos* is used, and this has led to a severe problem for theological vocabulary in many vernacular languages. The only word we have in English to express the meaning of *sacerdos*, "priest" (like the French *prêtre* and the German

Priester), is itself merely an abbreviation of the very different term, *presbyter*. This term, meaning "elder," was used in Greek to designate the members of the Jerusalem Sanhedrin and has always been the term applied to the second order of the Christian ministry. In spite of this, "priest" has been used so long and so consistently to render the Latin *sacerdos*, that we must say that its content is identical with the Latin term, and this can lead to anomalies.

I am happy to be Professor of Liturgics in The General Theological Seminary of the Episcopal Church. I received my own theological training here between 1948 and 1951, and returned for graduate study in 1961. I returned again to join the faculty in my present post in 1971. While the buildings of the seminary, like most in Manhattan, seem to be in a constant process of evolution, the chapel has changed less than most and has been a significant place for me for more than half my life. It is a rather grand example of Victorian collegiate gothic, most of whose decorative features are more Victorian than gothic. The plan, however, is decidedly collegiate if not monastic, the major space between the short ante-chapel and the spacious sanctuary being given to the long choir in which three ranks of stalls rise up on either side of the center aisle, with a further rank of stalls for the faculty at the top. On the wall above these, running the entire length of the chapel on both sides, is a band of dark stone in which are incised and gilded in Latin the words of the imperative formula of ordination in the *Book of Common Prayer*. It is, apart from the precisions added in 1662, this formula which we encounter in the Pontifical of William Durandus, where it is found accompanying a second imposition of hands after the concelebration and communion of the newly ordained.[1] The text is taken from John 20:22f.: *Accipe Spiritum Sanctum, quorum remiseris peccata remittuntur eis et quorum retinueris retenta erunt*. This was taken as basis of the ordination formula in the Anglican Ordinal of 1550, but it is the expanded text of 1662 that still confronts our students as it confronted me in 1948. Few incoming students today can appreciate much more than I the plangent periods of that nineteenth-century translation from English into Latin, but one word does shine out for most of them—as it did for me in my first year—to identify the goal before me and to sustain me in my trials. *Accipe Spiritum Sanctum*, it says, *in officium et opus* **Sacer-dotis** *in Ecclesia Dei*. The chapel was dedicated in 1888, and it would be eight more years before Leo XIII, then gloriously reigning, would express the views that would etch these words, *officium Sacerdotis*, still deeper in the hearts of Anglican seminarians. None then would know that, given the central and critical role and function of that formula in the ordination rite, it was *in this translation* not a claim upon the tradition but a radical departure from it. Whatever other texts have been added to illuminate or explicate the traditional rites of ordination to the second order of the hierarchy, these rites have continued at their sober center to speak not of any *officium Sacerdotis*, but rather, as does the Roman *praefatio*, of the *Presbyterii dignitatem*. There is, we now recognize, no one order of ministry in which the *sacerdotium Christi* is situated, though priesthood in that sense certainly pertains to the liturgical ministries of both the episcopate and presbyterate, as it does to the *ecclesia* over which they preside.

Baptism to Priesthood

Father Aidan Kavanagh, in a paper prepared for the Christian Initiation section of the 1979 meeting of the North American Academy of Liturgy, said:

> The sacerdotal community of the baptized needs ministers to serve its needs, but the presence of ministers exercising *sacerdotium* within it neither de-sacerdotalizes everyone else nor deprives the community at large of its corporate "ministry of reconciliation" in the world, nor does this reduce the baptized to the level of a proletariat composed of second-class citizens in the Church. Nothing could be more opposed to the deepest instincts of Catholic tradition than this. Yet the association of priesthood with the presbyterate among the western churches has presbyteralized not only the ministry but the very sacerdotality of the Church as well. This in turn has lent a certain ruthless logic to the pernicious perception of ordination to the presbyterate as the only way of achieving true Christian status, or even "first-class citizenship," in the Church. Our various seminaries are full of people seeking this apparent yet non-existent "honor." [2]

While I sincerely hope that there will be a great many who do not recognize the situation which Father Kavanagh describes, I must say that I do recognize it and have been troubled by it for years. I have watched generations of seminarians frown with disappointment at the lean and sparse theology of presbyterate in the ordination prayer of the third-century *Apostolic Tradition*, only to come alive with excitement at the description of the three-year catechumenate later in this document. They recognized themselves in the three-year formation process much more than they did in the ordination of the presbyter. He was simply selected by a process not described, and seems to have had no discernible preparation for the role beyond years of faithful and responsible Christian life and witness, so many years, indeed, that one might think of him as an elder. Such a one has little in common with students in a three-year formation process which they see as moving toward participation in the priesthood of Christ.

The recent revision of our liturgical rites has, if anything, sharpened the sting of this interplay of images between initiation and ordination. Shortly after the promulgation of the 1979 *Book of Common Prayer*, the infant son of one of our students was baptized in the seminary chapel by that student's bishop, and I was one of two presbyters assisting him. After the triple immersion and the clothing of the infant, the deacon with the paschal candle led us back to the sanctuary where, before the altar, the bishop recited the prayer before the seal and performed the chrismation, saying, "James, you are sealed by the Holy Spirit in Baptism and marked as Christ's own forever." Then, while the bishop held the child up high where all could see him, the bishop, presbyters, deacon, and all the congregation, most of whom were seminarians, shouted to that tiny boy, "We receive you into the household of God. Confess the faith of Christ crucified, proclaim his resurrection, and share with us in his eternal priesthood." At that moment, my eye turned to the chapel wall and fell on the words, *Accipe Spiritum Sanctum in officium et opus Sacerdotis*, and I shivered at the recognition of the vastness of the change which has come upon us in this past quarter century, and the vastness of the further questions raised by this change.

Priesthood and Order

One such question has been raised and responded to by our own church among others, namely, would that infant have participated in the *sacerdotium* of Christ had it been a girl, and, if so, how would that impinge upon her as a potential subject for ordination? Whereas the first part of that question can easily be answered in the affirmative, the second is far more problematic. While much of the rhetoric addressing the question has been concerned with the ministerial exercise of *sacerdotium*, one wonders if this is the proper form of the question. Once again, the church ordains deacons, presbyters, and bishops. Inherent in the presidential responsibility of bishops and presbyters is the ministerial exercise of *sacerdotium*, but this, however central, is but one dimension of those offices. Women, just as men, participate in Christ's eternal priesthood by baptism into his Body. Whether this marks any baptized person for *episkope* is a separate question. It is interesting that where there is no question of *episkope* as such, that is, in the diaconate, we can see the ordination of women in the earlier strata of the tradition, even though there is little question of *sacerdotium* in relation to this order. What significance are we to assign to the tradition's failure or refusal to assign oversight to women?

St. Thomas Aquinas, noting that Christ is the chief baptizer, will allow to women the ministry of baptism in cases of necessity on the basis of Galatians 3:38, so frequently quoted today in the context of the discussion of ordination, namely, "in Christ there is neither male nor female." It is not on any basis of woman's physical dissimilarity to the human Jesus, then, that he bases his opinion that women cannot be promoted to orders, but rather the conviction that women are subject by nature, the same ground on which he observes that women are not allowed to teach publicly (presumably meaning that women cannot be awarded the doctorate).[3]

Though one must have the deepest reverence for the powerful intellect of the Angelic Doctor, it must be confessed that a great many matters that he saw as *de natura* have turned out, in consequence of sociological, technological, political, and other developments, to be considerably more negotiable than he might have thought. It would require even more foolishness than I can muster to inform the Prime Minister of the United Kingdom that she is subject by nature, let aside to so address the one whose subject she is. Mrs. Thatcher is, of course, subject to God, but this is a dignity she shares with all humanity, male or female. While it is clear that she has been called to a position of responsibility to and authority over the political life of her nation, to what extent this will be true of women in the ecclesiastical sphere remains to the Holy Spirit to determine. The question is not whether a bishop can ordain a woman, finally, but whether the church will call a woman. Such an appreciation of vocation, however, is difficult for too many today.

Vocation and Order

Many centuries have accustomed us to the notion that vocation is born in the heart of the subject of vocation, but these many centuries have been fewer than we might think. Most ante-Nicene bishops would have been shocked, I dare say, at the thought of a young person "seeking Holy Orders," as we are today embarrassed, if not always shocked, at a presbyter overtly seeking the episcopate. In the case of the episcopate, the primitive notion of calling perseveres to a large extent. But today's seminarian has come to seek Holy Orders as the result of much inner searching and not infrequently in consequence of a profound experience of conversion. Whereas this spiritual experience is worthy of genuine rejoicing on the part of the church, in many ways the goal of this quest has more in common with monastic life than with the ancient presbyterate. We may recall that almost contemporaneous with the decline of the catechumenate, Theodore of Tarsus could say that all the Fathers called religious profession "a second baptism."[4] Catechumenate, as initiatory process, had given way to the novitiate, and (for all the differences between them) the novitiate would, in many traditions, give way to seminary formation, a process begun in the heart of the seminarian as it was in the heart of the fledgling friar or monk or hermit, and as it was yet earlier in one who heard the Gospel and sought holy baptism. When so many parts of the church are suffering for lack of vocations, it may seem odd to suggest that this represents a novel and perhaps distorted understanding of the nature of Holy Order. In other areas, however, vocations abound and, as Father Kavanagh suggested, it is often difficult to be sure that that vocation is not simply to Christian life. I have not attempted to ascertain the point at which the initiative in the matter of vocation moved from the Spirit guiding the church to the Spirit moving the heart of the Christian individual, though Innocent III's order that bishops must supply alimentation to any priests ordained without title suggests that the problem is at least that old. The title of *patrimonii sui* surely marked a further gain for the notion of absolute ordination. Certainly the Reformation insistence on vocation to a particular congregation was a bold step toward recovering the primitive priorities, but this itself has begun to soften as pastors find themselves drawn into non-pastoral responsibilities in ecclesiastical administration, higher education, social service agencies, and the like. It would be archaeological romanticism to expect the pastors of established congregations to be ordained to the presbyterate only to assume leadership of that congregation, just as it would be to expect that we shall soon see again the ordination of a Bishop of Rome. But it seems to me that the notion of ordination to title is in trouble, and less than responsible outcries about the "right to ordination" testify to this. The really foolish notion of a "right to ordination" betrays a lingering conviction that one participates in the *sacerdotium Christi* only by ordination to presbyterate, and the sorrow is not that some Christians believe that they should share in the priesthood of Christ, but that the presbyteral hegemony has too long closed our eyes to the fact that all do.

Toward Clarity

We have all known all along the New Testament texts that speak of the sacerdotality of the church and also the tradition's regular reiteration of that profound truth, fundamental to both ecclesiology and Christology; but preoccupation with *sacerdotium* as a *potestas* conferred at ordination to presbyterate left us disinclined to afford this truth the full articulation it needs. At times, indeed, the notion of the priesthood of the faithful was believed by some to contain the seeds, at least, of anticlericalism. The reformers never taught the presbyterate of all believers, but others failed to teach the presbyterate of all presbyters,[5] and in the light of this failure we have been hard put to understand or give structural expression to the relation of presbyterate to episcopate and the relation of diaconate to both, and the relation of all to the life of the total Body of Christ, our High Priest.

A particular problem which faces those whose work it is to speak and write of these things is the failure of many of our vernacular languages to provide even the terms that reproduce the Latin's clear distinction between *presbyter* and *sacerdos* or their Greek counterparts. If we cannot devise linguistic conventions which will reproduce these distinctions, then—harsh as it may sound—we are incapable of communicating the tradition. If a given language does allow the distinction (as does our retention of both presbyter and priest) and we fail to distinguish consistently, then—harsh as it may sound—we fail to communicate the tradition. Much of the work of those engaged in liturgical formation will entail the loving courtship of ambiguity, but ambiguity is not equivocation, nor is it obfuscation. If we can admit that the tradition has consistently spoken of the ordination of presbyters, then the recognition that we are baptized into priesthood will cause little confusion, even when we recognize, as we must, that the authorized liturgical president—presbyter or bishop—plays a distinctive and necessary role in the exercise of the church's priesthood. Behind the sacerdotal duties of ordained ministers stands the sacerdotal character of the church, and behind this stands the high priest of the New Covenant himself, Jesus Christ, who calls us in a vast variety of ministries—some pastors, some preachers, some teachers, or bishops, or vardapeds, or cantors, or deacons, or hegoumenoi, or ushers, or presbyters, or just saints—to be his peculiar people, a holy nation, a kingdom of priests to serve our God.

Notes

1. M. Andrieu, *Le Pontifical romain au moyen-âge*, vol. 3, Studi e Testi, vol. 88 (Citta del Vaticano, 1940) 372.
2. *Worship* 53:4 (1979) 336.
3. *Summa Theol.* III.67.4.
4. *Poenitentiale*, cap. iii (PL 99:928).

5. Even in our recent past the provisional translation of the ordination rites issued by ICEL in 1969 rendered the crucial phrase in the ordination prayer, *presbyterii dignitatem*, as "the dignity of the presbyterate." This brought storms of protest, and the translation quickly became "the dignity of the priesthood."

2

Sources and Structures
of the Eucharistic Prayer

EVEN BEFORE FRANK GAVIN'S 1928 LECTURES ON *JEWISH ANTECEDENTS of the Christian Sacraments*,[1] it was common for exegetes to identify the Greek terms *eucharistia* and *eulogia* and to see both as translations of the Hebrew *berakah*, "benediction," encouraging efforts to see the roots of the Christian eucharist in Jewish prayer forms. With greater intensity since the seminal essay of Jean-Paul Audet at the Oxford Conference on the Four Gospels in 1957,[2] a growing body of scholarship on the eucharist has focused on the literary structure of the eucharistic prayer and its relation to Jewish euchology in the first century of the Common Era. Although the corpus of scholarly discourse has not yielded easy agreement on all disputed points, there is today a significant consensus that in this, as in many other matters, Christian liturgy needs to be seen against its Jewish backgrounds, where these backgrounds can be recovered with any precision.

Eucharist and Meal Grace

Like many before him, but in greater detail, Audet studied the prayer form that he took to be fundamental to all Jewish euchology, the benediction (*berakah*), and sought to find in the structure of what he called the "cultic *berakah*" (the benediction followed by the motive of the praise and concluded by another short benediction as doxology) the pattern that would give rise to the Christian eucharistic prayer.

In fact, it now seems clear that the form of the benediction to which Audet appealed was unknown in the first century and was, even in the rabbinic prescriptions of the third century, but one of several forms of prayer encountered in Jewish euchology. We are now familiar with a collection of hymns among the Dead Sea Scrolls, virtually all of which are hymns or psalms of thanksgiving that make no use of the standard opening of the benediction. Further, Robert Ledogar attacked Audet's too easy identification of *berakah* and *eucharistia*,[3] an identification that was virtually standard among exegetes and liturgists even before Audet,[4] but given greater impetus by his study.

Both Louis Bouyer and Louis Ligier, again, pointed to the importance of the structure of the Jewish meal grace, *Birkat Ha-Mazon*, in which an initial benediction is followed by a thanksgiving (beginning *nodeh lekah*, "we give thanks to you"), and a supplication for Israel, yielding a series of three prayers rather than the single form to which Audet appealed.[5] While it has been suggested that such a complex of prayer might well have been used by Jesus at the Last Supper, the impact of such a euchological pattern on the Christian eucharistic prayer would not depend upon the imitation of an act of Jesus, but on the place of such a meal grace in the Judaic tradition to which primitive Christianity belonged.

In a paper read at the congress of *Societas Liturgica* in Trier in 1975,[6] I came to the conclusion that the Christian eucharistic prayer is not derived directly from the Jewish *berakah* form, the benediction whose principal verbal root is *brk*, but rather that it is related to prayers such as *nodeh lekah*, thanksgivings whose operative verb is a form of the root *ydh*, and that it is that Hebrew verb that is encountered in Greek as *eucharistein*. Following leads from Louis Finkelstein and Louis Ligier, I argued that chapter 10 of *Didache* shows us an adaptation of *Birkat Ha-Mazon* to the distinctive table rite of Christians. In this group of prayers (to be said after communion, evidently) the initial *berakah* of the Jewish formulae is not found and the series begins with a thanksgiving reminiscent of the second pericope of the Jewish grace, *nodeh lekah*. Echos of the content of the missing opening benediction are found in a second thanksgiving, and the series concludes with a supplication for the church similar to that for Israel in the Jewish forms. At the conclusion of that essay, having summed up my disagreement with the attempts of Audet and others to establish the equivalence of *berakah* and *eucharistia*, I expressed the hope that further studies would help us to understand better the significance and consequences of such a reassessment.

More Recent Developments

Several developments since 1975 have sustained this hope and have contributed to the picture available now of the shape of Jewish euchology in the days before the destruction of the temple, a picture which contributes significantly to our understanding of the early development of eucharistic prayers.

One such major improvement in the resources available to us today is the translation of Joseph Heinemann's important study of *Prayer in the Period of the Amoraim and the Tannaim*. This work, in modern Hebrew, was published in 1966, but appeared in a slightly revised form and in English in 1977 under the title, *Prayer in the Talmud*.[7] Here Heinemann argues persuasively that the *berakah*, which would become so central a prayer form in the Amoraic period, had been, in its biblical background, not a prayer addressed to God at all, but a praise of God stated in the third person. By analogy we might think of the credal formularies in Christian liturgical literature. New Testament examples of such "biblical *berakoth*", to use Heinemann's phrase, can be seen still in such New Testament texts as Luke 1:68, Ephesians 1:3, and 1 Peter 1:3. That these are benedictions of God is clear, but they differ from what we might understand to be prayer forms in that they are not addressed to God, but rather speak *of* God, having their pronouns and verb forms in the third person.

By contrast to such benedictions, Heinemann notes that there are other forms that are addressed to God, such as prayers of thanksgiving, of confession, or of supplication. The rising importance attached to the *berakah* form later, he believes, led to the addition of brief benedictions to the ends of such prayers which were addressed to God, a concluding "eulogy" (as Heinemann's translation calls it) or *chatimah* ("seal"). Heinemann describes the function of this brief formula: "by means of its use it becomes possible to transform any prayer, whatever its style, into a 'liturgical' prayer with a standard form . . . since not all prayers are conducive to opening in the *Baruk*-style."[8] Nonetheless, being added to a prayer addressed to God, this concluding *chatimah* was also addressed to God, for example, "Blessed are you, O Lord, for the land and for the food."

Eventually, this form of address was adopted even for the older *berakoth*, but only for the opening phrase, yielding one of the more curious characteristics of the Jewish liturgical *berakah*-form, an opening address to God in the second person, which then shifts to the (original) third person forms for verbs and pronouns in the body of the benediction, as, for example, "Blessed are you, YHWH our God, King of the universe, who feeds the world with goodness . . ." This structurally significant characteristic of liturgical *berakoth*, a vestige, Heinemann believes, of their originally consistent third person form, is often unnoticed by commentators since it has long been customary to smooth out translations by using second person forms throughout, effectively destroying this significant euchological evidence. Ledogar's cavillation at Audet's too easy identification of *berakah* and *eucharistia* dealt primarily with those two words, but the work of Heinemann shows that the problem is really more profound. If we are talking about prayer structures, then the difference between the benediction form and the thanksgiving form goes far beyond the semantic difference of the two words, "benediction" and "thanksgiving."

While Heinemann dates both the addition of the *chatimah* and the consequent rephrasing of the address of the *berakah* to the period of the second temple, a text from a work of the end of the second century B.C., *The Book of Jubilees*, reveals the shape of things prior to those changes, suggesting either a knowledgeable archaism on the part of the author or, more probably, a *terminus post quem* for the standardization of the developments detailed by Heinemann, a process that he believes continued into our era. Standardization, even of structures, moves slowly. Verbal variation, beyond this, is constant in prayer tradition and was still rife in these prayers in the Middle Ages. Indeed, a chief accomplishment of Heinemann's work is to show that the supposed "original text" of *Birkat Ha-Mazon*, sought by Finkelstein, had never existed.

A comparison of *Jubilees* 22:5-9 to the developed texts of *Birkat Ha-Mazon* in the siddurim of the gaonic period shows not only interesting differences in content, but also an impressive similarity of structure. Even so, the opening benediction in *Jubilees* is in the third person throughout, and the following thanksgiving and supplication lack the *chatimoth*, the brief benedictions that are found attached to them later. These prayers in *Jubilees* are presented as a grace recited by Abraham after eating a "thank offering" (*zebach todah?*) sent to him from Isaac by the hand of Jacob.

> [5]And Isaac also sent by the hand of Jacob a good thank offering to Abraham so that he might eat and drink. [6]And he ate and drank and blessed God Most High who created heaven and earth and who made all the fat of the earth and gave it to the sons of man so that they might eat and drink and bless their Creator. [7]"And now I thank you, my God, because you have let me see this day. Behold, I am one hundred and seventy-five years old, and fulfilled in days. And all of my days were peaceful for me. [8]The sword of the enemy did not triumph over me in anything which you gave to me or my sons all the days of my life until this day. [9]O my God, may your mercy and your peace be upon your servant and upon the seed of his sons so that they might become an elect people for you and an inheritance from all the nations of the earth from henceforth and for all the days of the generations of the earth forever." [9]

The author's concern to avoid overt anachronism makes the content of these prayers placed on the lips of Abraham differ significantly from the later forms. Here the thanksgiving is focused on God's protection of his gifts to Abraham and his sons from "the sword of the enemy", while the equivalent prayer in the later text gives thanks for the promised land and for the gift of Torah. Similarly, the supplication in *Jubilees* 22:9 asks mercy and peace upon Abraham and the seed of his sons, while the text in the siddurim asks protection for Israel, and also prays for the building of Jerusalem and the establishment of the Kingdom of David.

Thanksgiving for Salvation

Heinemann notes that the initial benediction of the meal grace has universal reference, speaking of God as Creator of all, whereas the thanksgiving has a more particular historical reference to God's gifts to the people of the Covenant. The following supplication is oriented toward the future of the people. Of these three concerns, Heinemann says:

> Throughout the liturgy, we find repeatedly juxtaposed the three basic and complementary motifs of Creation—Revelation (viz., the Giving of the Torah)—Redemption, which in the Rabbinic world-view mark respectively the beginning of the history of mankind, the critical turning-point in the progression of that history, and the ultimate goal and final destination of the historical continuum.[10]

Christian theology, of course, would designate this "critical turning-point" differently, recognizing Jesus as the Messiah who has already inaugurated the "Redemption" whose future consummation is, nonetheless, "the ultimate goal and final destination of the historical continuum." One is tempted, nonetheless, to see a very similar triad of concerns in the Syro-Byzantine anaphoras of the fourth and fifth centuries where an opening praise of God as Creator, ending in the *Sanctus*, leads to a thanksgiving for the revelation of salvation in the work of Christ, itself followed by a supplication for the outpouring of the Holy Spirit upon the community.

As attractive as one might find such a similarity, there is reason to doubt that a direct structural continuity exists between these Christian anaphoras and the *Birkat Ha-Mazon*. The anaphora of the *Apostolic Tradition* from the third century lacks this initial passage focused on the Creator and its concluding angelic hymn.[11] After an initial dialogue, which includes the bidding, "Let us give thanks," the *Apostolic Tradition*'s eucharistic prayer opens directly with the Christological thanksgiving, a recounting of the incarnation and work of Christ climaxed by the account of the institution of the eucharist and the memorial oblation of the gifts in thanksgiving. This extended thanksgiving is followed by a supplication for the outpouring of the Spirit upon the offering of the community. Such a bipartite structure, consisting of only thanksgiving and supplication, is not limited to the isolated example of the *Apostolic Tradition*. The same structure is found in an anaphora of the fourth or fifth century ascribed to Epiphanius.[12]

When the bipartite (thanksgiving-supplication) structure is compared with the prayers of chapters 9 and 10 of *Didache*, one perceives in these earlier texts as well the preference for thanksgiving language to which attention has been called above. In both chapters, two thanksgivings, each with a doxology, are followed by a supplication, also with a doxology. The prayers in chapter 9 precede the distribution, and so might be viewed as corresponding to the short *berakoth* before and during a Jewish meal. It cannot be categorically said that thanksgivings such as those in chapter 9 never replaced the more familiar benedictions. However, nothing that we know of Jewish meal prayers would prepare us for a supplication before eating such as that in *Didache* 9:4. It seems better, then, to think of the prayers in chapter 9 as modelled on those of chapter 10, themselves derived from *Birkat Ha-Mazon*.

In spite of much scholarly argument over whether the prayers in these two chapters of *Didache* are for a eucharist, an agape, for both of those, or represent a conversion of one to the other, there seems to be no compelling reason to take the prayers as intended for anything other than a very primitive eucharist.[13] Chapter 10, following the tradition of Jewish meal prayer, would come after eating and drinking, that is, after the distribution of bread and wine. The replication of its structure to provide, prior to the distribution, thanksgivings over the cup and bread and a supplication for the church could be understood to represent a very early recognition that the special character of this meal fellowship requires prayer over the gifts prior to their distribution, a concern continued in all the anaphoral tradition.

There remains the question of the reason for the structural difference between *Birkat Ha-Mazon* and *Didache* 10. The opening thanksgiving in chapter 10 of the *Didache*, as we noted above, is reminiscent of the thanksgiving, *nodeh lekah*, which is the second of the Jewish forms. Here we can see the same sort of response to God's distinctive gifts to his covenanted people. What is missing in *Didache* is the initial, more universally extended benediction of

God as Creator of all and provider of food to all, Israelite and non-Israelite alike. That blessing of God as food-giver is transformed in *Didache* 10:3 into a second thanksgiving for the gifts of spiritual food and drink and eternal life, for food and drink that have been assimilated to the covenant relationship, no longer merely the alimentation provided for all by the Creator.

> You, almighty Master, created all things for the sake of your Name, and gave food and drink to mankind for their enjoyment [that they might give you thanks][14]; but to us you have granted spiritual food and drink and eternal life through your child Jesus. Above all we give you thanks because you are mighty; glory to you for evermore.

The food and drink of the eucharist belong to that "historical-particularistic element," to use Heinemann's phrase, which we might characterize as the economy of salvation. As the thanksgiving of the Jewish meal grace, *nodeh lekah*, gave thanks for (*inter alia*) "your covenant which you have sealed in our flesh," so *Didache* 10 gives thanks for "your holy Name which you have enshrined in our hearts," but also for the spiritual food and drink that are now distinguished from the food and drink given to all people for their enjoyment, the physical nourishment for which the initial *berakah* of the Jewish grace blessed the universal Creator. This primitive Christian recasting of the grace after meals reflects the understanding that this cultic meal is the supper of the Lord, which Paul labored to distinguish from the ordinary alimentation that he urged the Corinthians to take at home (1 Cor 11:20-22, 34). This revision explains why Christian tradition has so consistently spoken of the center of its worship as the eucharist, thanksgiving, not the eulogy or the benediction. *Didache* 14, further, speaks of the eucharist as a sacrifice, citing Malachi 1:11, and in my earlier paper in 1975 I noted the use of eucharistic language in a sacrificial context by Hellenistic Jewish writers, as shown by such scholars as Henri Cazelles and Jean LaPorte.[15]

Giraudo's Alternative

An alternative explanation for the prevalence of "thanksgiving" language was given some years ago by Cesare Giraudo, arguing radically that this characteristic of Christian prayer is in continuity with the Old Testament and demonstrates, in fact, the very slight influence of rabbinic euchological development on early Christianity.[16] Giraudo's work, his doctoral dissertation at the Pontifical Gregorian University, defended in 1980, is divided into three parts. The first is concerned with "the Old Testament *tôdâ*," the second with the Jewish *berakah*, and the third with the Christian anaphora.

Central to Giraudo's argument is his identification of a literary structure in formulae related to the formation or maintenance of the covenant relationship, to the euchological form of which he assigns the term *tôdâ*. These formulae may relate to the formation of the covenant between Israel and God, to the violation of the terms of that covenant, or to the restoration of the covenant. Central to the character of such a formula is the dual value of the verb root *ydh*, which can mean either "confess" in the sense of proclamation (as we speak of a "confession of faith"), or an admission of wrongdoing, a confession of sin. The first of these two senses of *ydh* is that which is continued most often in Christian Greek as *eucharistein*. While *ydh* can be translated into English as "confess," it is the verb that gives their common name to the "thanksgiving psalms" at Qumran. Giraudo's *tôdâ* formulae fall into two parts. The first is a recounting of God's actions on Israel's behalf; the second, after a ligature such as "and now" or "therefore", lodges the community's supplication for God's further action on its behalf. Even in discussing Old Testament texts, Giraudo, somewhat anachronistically, designates these two parts of his *tôdâ* as "anamnetic" and "epicletic."

Either of those two parts can provide the context for a further element in his structure, the "embolism", a literary figure, inserted in the manner of a scripture citation, which serves as *locus theologicus* of the entire formula. This "embolism" is accorded particularly high importance in the third part of Giraudo's study, being identified there with the narrative of the institution of the eucharist. Giraudo, indeed, classifies all eucharistic prayers on the basis of the location of this narrative in either the anamnetic or epicletic part of the prayer.[17]

He points to two allusions to the psalms in the opening benediction of the meal grace (in the Italian rite) as anamnetic embolisms, but his attempts to identify such embolisms in the *berakoth* are limited by his radical insistence that the rabbinic benedictions represent a late addition to a euchological tradition rooted in the Old Testament *tôdâ*, rather than in the biblical *berakoth* of which Heinemann speaks. Consequently, he fails to discern the opening benediction in the grace of Abraham in *Jubilees* 22:6, and treats the second and third segments of that grace, the thanksgiving and supplication, as a single bipartite prayer, an example of his *tôdâ-*form. The later addition of *chatimoth* between the thanksgiving and supplication of *Birkat Ha-Mazon* and also at the conclusion of the supplication he views as a distortion of the original continuous prayer. The series of *berakoth* encountered in later Jewish euchology, therefore, simply results from the insertion of these short benedictions (*chatimoth*), a process of codification over a long period, completed only in the Babylonian academies. In the *stato attuale dei testi*, he says, it is only those *chatimoth* that allow us to speak of a long formulary as a series of *berakoth*.[18]

Such a reassessment of the development of Jewish euchology might not concern us were it not for Giraudo's conviction that his Old Testament *tôdâ* passed on into Christian liturgy with but slight influence from the rabbinic forms and patterns. In the final chapter of his consideration of Jewish *berakoth*, Giraudo examines the Jewish-Christian formularies that are closely related to Judaic forms. Two of these, *Didache* 10 and *Apostolic Constitutions* VII. 26.2-4, Giraudo entitles *La Birkat Hammazon Cristiana*. However, in spite of the division of *Didache* 10 into three sections, each concluded with a doxology, Giraudo speaks of its *nettamente struttura bipartita*, and presents the text without a break between the first two paragraphs, while an open line separates those thanksgiving forms from the supplicatory third paragraph, a format that heightens the similarity of the text to that of *Apostolic Constitutions* VII.26 on the facing page. This later form of the text, no longer divided by doxologies and with the expression *kai nun* effecting the transition from thanksgiving to supplication, provides (apart from the question of the "embolism") an excellent example of the *tôdâ* as Giraudo describes it, a continuous bipartite prayer of thanksgiving and supplication. Such later recasting, however, does not account for the division of the original text in *Didache* 10 into three sections by its three doxologies, a structural characteristic that suggests a stronger influence of the tripartite Jewish text than Giraudo is prepared to accept. Part II of the dissertation concludes with a long excursus on the semantic value of *eucharistein*.

It is in Part III of his dissertation that Giraudo turns his attention to the anaphora, and, as noted above, he here identifies the "embolism" of his *tôdâ* structure with the institution narrative and develops an anaphoral taxonomy based on the position assigned to the institution narrative, whether in the celebrative/anamnetic first part of the anaphora or in the supplicatory/epicletic second part. To the first type belong the pseudo-Clementine anaphora of *Apostolic Constitutions* VIII, the anaphora in the *Apostolic Tradition*, those of James, Chrysostom and Basil, and (much more guardedly) anaphoras of the Hispano-Gallican tradition. In all these the institution narrative and the anamnesis (*stricte dictu*) come as the climax to a more or less extended Christological thanksgiving.

Anaphoras of the second type, however, arrive at the institution narrative and anamnesis only after the prayer has moved into a supplicatory (epicletic) mode. Among the anaphoras of this type Giraudo numbers the East Syrian Anaphora of the Apostles (Addai and Mari and its Maronite parallel, *Sharar*), the Egyptian anaphoras of Serapion and of St. Mark, and the Roman Canon.

Whereas the first type probably represents a genuine historical continuity in the tradition of the eucharistic prayer, the second group appears to reflect only a single structural similarity among prayers between which it is difficult to draw significant historical connections. Are we to envision historical continuity, direct or indirect, between East Syria and Rome? What would be the paths taken by such a tradition? Giraudo fails to ask this question, as he prescinds from questions of historical precision throughout. His concern is only with literary structure, but we must question whether such a limited concern can yield a scientifically useful taxonomy. Is it really useful simply to divide all anaphoras into two types, one of which includes both the Anaphora of Addai and Mari and the Roman Canon?

Further, especially after we have introduced the East Syrian and Syro-Byzantine traditions into the discussion, it becomes necessary to observe that Giraudo's bipartite schema becomes at many points a procrustean bed. This was already evident in his treatment of *Didache* 10 and its three doxologies, but it arises again in the face of the three *gehanata* of the Anaphora of the Apostles and the similar tripartite structure encountered in the Syro-Byzantine prayers with their opening praise of the Creator ending in the *Sanctus*.

Role of the Sanctus

New developments in the years during and immediately following Giraudo's research throw some light on questions he could not address and also call some of his conclusions into fresh question. In 1980 Bryan Spinks published his study of Jewish sources for the *Sanctus* which, to my mind, set this problem in a much clearer context than had been done previously.[19] In what was hardly more than an aside, he asked why eucharistic prayers, grown out of the Jewish tradition of table grace that had never known the *Sanctus* (*Kedushah*), should adopt this hymn, so rooted in the synagogue liturgy.

Several studies had previously sought to relate the anaphora to the benedictions before Shema in the morning liturgy, with special reference to *Yotzer Or* and the *Sanctus* it introduces.[20] Those suggestions confronted Mann's early study of the published Cairo Genizah fragments that cast strong doubt on the occurrence of *Yotzer* and its *Kedushah* in the early Palestinian service.[21] But it was the appearance of Heinemann's work, again, that drew attention to further studies in modern Hebrew based on unpublished Genizah fragments that overthrow Mann's findings and thus reopen the question of synagogue influence on the anaphora.[22]

Hansjörg Auf der Maur's study of the paschal homilies of Asterios had in 1967 called attention to the appearance of the *Sanctus* in both non-eucharistic and eucharistic contexts in the first half of the fourth century.[23] This suggested the needed bridge between the synagogue and the table prayers. It seems possible, at least to me, that the Aramaic speaking Christian synagogue had adopted forms of praise including the *Sanctus* for its morning service, precursors to such forms as we find in *Apostolic Constitutions* VII.35, and that it was from such Christian usage rather than directly from the synagogue in Judaism that such a praise of the Creator ending in the *Sanctus* entered the anaphoral tradition.[24]

Also in 1980, William Macomber presented to the Dumbarton Oaks symposium, "East of Byzantium," his reconstruction of the common source of both the Anaphora of Addai and Mari and the third Maronite Anaphora of Peter (*Sharar*). Here he restated more strongly than he had in 1971 his conviction that the absence of the institution narrative from Addai and Mari was the result of a reform under Isho-Yabh III in the seventh century, and that *Sharar* at that point represents the common source, the Anaphora of the Apostles.[25] It is possible to see in his text a bipartite form, beginning after the *Sanctus*, which could have been independent from the very primitive opening prayer that comes to its conclusion in the *Sanctus*.[26] The prayer after the *Sanctus* begins, "We give thanks to you, O Lord, we your sinful servants because you have effected in us your grace which cannot be repaid."[27] Such a bipartite form would be quite similar structurally to the anaphora of the *Apostolic Tradition*, save for the situation of the institution narrative in the supplicatory section. Nonetheless, there is no compelling indication of a seam after the *Sanctus* in Macomber's reconstructed text, and this text (albeit a reconstruction of an extinct original) may very well present to us the earliest appearance of the *Sanctus* in a Christian anaphora, coming as it does out of the strongly Jewish-Christian environment of Aramaic-speaking East Syria. There seems no reason why such a tripartite prayer could not belong to the third century and, indeed, to any point in that century. For that reason, to insist, as Giraudo does, on fitting the received texts of the Syrian anaphoras to a two-part scheme seriously oversimplifies the data.[28]

This said, it may well be that a bipartite prayer lies behind the three-fold structure in which we encounter these texts. In the original form of this chapter,[29] I suggested that the *Sanctus* hymn, with the opening prayer which it concludes, marked a new development in the tradition of the eucharistic prayer in the East, adding a theological section to the two-part Christological thanksgiving and pneumatological supplication such as we see in the *Apostolic Tradition*. Something very close to this development can be traced in a later anaphora preserved in Syriac.

Reference has been made above to an anaphora attributed to Epiphanius of Salamis, which has the same thanksgiving-supplication structure as the prayer of *Apostolic Tradition*, a structure lacking both a theological section and the *Sanctus*.[30] The year following Garitte's publication of this text, Hieronymus Engberding noted the incorporation and expansion of the Anaphora of Epiphanius in the Syriac Anaphora of Timotheus of Alexandria.[31] The Anaphora of Timotheus opens with an extensive praise of God as Creator leading into the *Sanctus*, and it is only after that hymn that the parallels to Epiphanius (and others to the Syriac James) occur. Although we are dealing here with texts from the fifth century at the earliest, this does show the extension of a bipartite to a tripartite prayer by prefixing a theological prayer ending in the *Sanctus* and can suggest that the same process had occurred earlier.

At the very least, it would seem that the search for the origins of the *Sanctus* in the anaphora should seek it as the conclusion of a prayer to which it is integral. If the *Sanctus* was at some point (probably in the fifth century) inserted in Italy between the variable *Vere dignum* and the *canon actionis*, this need not mean that it entered the entire Christian tradition as only a hymn inserted into an integral prayer that had previously lacked it. Such an insertion of the *Sanctus* at Rome was only one way in which liturgies that had not known the hymn adopted it from other traditions.

The addition of a praise of the Creator (leading into the *Sanctus*) to the beginning of a thanksgiving-supplication bipartite prayer would afford an explanation of the relationship between the bipartite anaphora of the *Apostolic Tradition* and the tripartite Antiochene or Syro-Byzantine anaphoras. There, however, the *Sanctus* seems in most cases to have occasioned the suppression of the opening thanksgiving verb of the following Christological prayer by repeated extension of the "Holy" of the angelic hymn. Further, the *eucharistēsōmen* of the dialogue led eventually to the addition of thanksgiving verbs to the opening theological praise. Nonetheless, this does not obscure the close similarity of the Christological section following the *Sanctus* to the opening thanksgiving of *Apostolic Tradition*. The classical Syro-Byzantine form seems to have appeared before 300, the time to which it is believed we can trace the origins of the Alexandrian text of the anaphora of Basil, the normal anaphora of the Coptic Church today.[32]

The Alexandrian Tradition

It is fascinating to find this prayer identified with Alexandria, given the often noted differences between Alexandrian prayers and that Syro-Byzantine form. The different structure at Alexandria presents an opening praise of the Creator through Christ, oblation of sacrifice in thanksgiving, and intercessory supplications, all prior to the *Sanctus*. After this hymn, there follows a still supplicatory connection to the institution narrative and (*stricte dictu*) anamnesis, its expression of oblation in the past tense. The anamnesis leads, in the extant complete texts, to a consecratory epiklesis and the concluding doxology.

Attempts since Vatican II to introduce a pneumatological consecratory epiklesis prior to the institution narrative of the Latin rite have frequently claimed roots in the Alexandrian tradition for such a consecratory prayer. In the new Roman eucharistic prayers, a consecratory epiklesis is situated prior to the narrative, a position analogous to the Roman Canon's *Quam oblationem*, and, after the anamnesis, there is a second epiklesis on the communicants.[33] Such an arrangement, however, is not to be found in any of the Alexandrian documents. One late fragment (sixth or seventh century) from Dêr Balyzeh, representing a local use, does make the connection from the *Sanctus* to the institution narrative a consecratory epiklesis, but, because the fragment breaks off just after the institution narrative, we know nothing of the content of any second epiklesis in that fragment, if there was one, nor do we know how the consecratory epiklesis affected the anamnesis. By contrast, it is the epiklesis following the institution narrative and anamnesis that is clearly consecratory in the anaphoras of Serapion and of Saint Mark.[34]

It was long common to suggest that the Alexandrian consecratory epiklesis following the anamnesis was the result of West Syrian influence. In recent years, however, several writers have suggested more radically that the entire "Alexandrian" anaphoral structure from *Sanctus* to final doxology is the result of such influence. Prior to that influence, according to this view, the Alexandrian eucharistic prayer had the much more primitive form preserved to us in Strasbourg papyrus 254.[35] There, in close parallel to the Liturgy of Saint Mark, an opening praise of God as Creator through Christ leads to the oblation of the sacrifice of thanksgiving over which intercessory supplications are offered. At the conclusion of these extended intercessions, the developed Liturgy of Saint Mark builds the introduction to the *Sanctus*, but in the Strasbourg papyrus there is instead what seems clearly to be a concluding doxology, making this very simple prayer a complete anaphora.

So described without further comment by Edward Kilmartin in 1974,[36] the understanding of the Strasbourg papyrus as a complete anaphora was explored more fully by Geoffrey Cuming in the Liturgy Master Theme at the Oxford Patristic Conference in 1979.[37] Two years later, a similar assertion of the integrity of the Strasbourg prayer by Herman Wegman suggested that the source of the Antiochene influence was the Liturgy of Saint James.[38]

However we understand the process of embellishment that produced the expanded Anaphora of St. Mark, there is good reason to see in Strasbourg 254 just such a bipartite eucharistic prayer as the *tôdâ* of which Giraudo speaks. Here is the "anamnetic" praise and thanksgiving for creation through Christ which leads into the "epicletic" intercessions for both living and departed. Still another recent writer, accepting but not pressing the integrity of the prayer in the papyrus, could say:

> Just as the intercessions of the Strasbourg Papyrus are not to be seen as an afterthought or intrusion, but are firmly set in the context of the thanksgiving that precedes them, so in the intercessions themselves the thread of the *eucharistia* is not lost, but is carried right through to the conclusion of the prayer. It ends where we have been taught to seek its ending, in the prayers of the saints and the worship of heaven.[39]

Although Giraudo sought to find in Addai and Mari material that would be equivalent to the absent institution narrative, and thus satisfy his structure's demand for this "embolism," Macomber's work argues that the narrative did appear in the common source of Addai and Mari and *Sharar*. Here in the Strasbourg papyrus, however, there is no such narrative nor any reference to Christ's institution of the eucharist. If we are to seek here an "embolism" that is characterized by a *citazione scritturistica in stile diretto* and which functions as *locus theologicus della domanda* (Giraudo, p. 170), then we must find it in the citation of Malachi 1:11, a citation that fits quite precisely Giraudo's description of his "embolism."

> ... Giving thanks through him to you with him and the Holy Spirit, we offer the reasonable sacrifice and this bloodless service, which all the nations offer you, "from sunrise to sunset," from south to north, [for] your "name is great among the nations, and in every place incense is offered to your holy name and a pure sacrifice." Over this sacrifice and offering we pray and beseech you ... [40]

Giraudo himself, of course, did not have access to these studies arguing the integrity of the Strasbourg papyrus, and consequently he does not treat the opening of St. Mark (prior to the *Sanctus*) as exhibiting all the characteristics of his *tôdâ* form. Rather, he seeks those characteristics in the later extended form of Mark, and so is at considerable pains to rationalize the appearance of the intercessions within what he regards as the anamnetic section of the prayer. He discusses that problem in the anaphora of Serapion, but deals with the much more extended intercessions before the *Sanctus* in St. Mark by the simple expedient of omitting them from the text, leaving only an ellipsis (p. 342) to represent almost a hundred lines of the prayer (in the format in *Prex Eucharistica*; 120 lines in that of Brightman).

It is, of course, only the introduction to the *Sanctus* (from line 19 in Giraudo's text on p. 342) that forces him to view these intercessions as a digression within the anamnetic portion of the prayer. In Strasbourg 254, on the other hand, the (evidently) final doxology stands in the place of this introduction to the *Sanctus*. The preceding intercessions are, to use Giraudo's terminology, the *sezione epicletica* of what Cuming, Wegman, and others view as the original prayer. Indeed, since it now seems likely that the claim for Mark's mission in Alexandria is at least as old as Clement,[41] this very primitive anaphora may already have been called the Anaphora of St. Mark before it was expanded by the introduction to the *Sanctus* and all that follows. Such a prayer, apart from certain of the petitions in the intercessions (e.g., for the army), could reach back to the second century. However, it would not be such an *anafora epicletica* as Giraudo makes the extended Mark. Rather, it was of Giraudo's first type in which the "embolism" falls within the anamnetic section, but that embolism is not the institution narrative. Rather, it is Malachi 1:11, a text cited in the context of the eucharist by *Didache* 14, Justin, and others.

Giraudo does not comment on that text, still found in the expanded St. Mark, or on its identification of the eucharist as a sacrifice. This is consistent with Giraudo's general but inexplicable diffidence regarding sacrifice, noted by several reviewers.[42] He rejects quite out of hand the studies of Laporte and Cazelles, which examine the sacrificial context of the use of eucharistic language by Jewish writers in Greek,[43] and minimizes (pp. 265-269) the connection between the *tôdâ* form he adumbrates and the *zebach todah*, the "sacrifice of thanksgiving" so frequently mentioned in the Old Testament. In this latter connection, Albert Gerhards calls attention to a 1977 work of H. Gese which was not used by Giraudo, but which promises to supply a better cultic context for his literary analysis.[44]

Conclusions

While, therefore, some important work has been done and is being done on the early history of the eucharistic prayer, it must be said that Giraudo's work fails to break new ground as far as the anaphoras themselves are concerned. The principal cause for this failure, it seems to me, is that he called upon his initial structural insight to bear more weight than it could. This closed his eyes to the initial benediction in *Jubilees* 22:6, to the doxologies in *Didache* 10, to the three rubrically indicated *qanone* that mark the tripartite structure of the Anaphora of the Apostles, to the structural differences between the eucharistic prayer of the *Apostolic Tradition* and the Syro-Byzantine anaphoras effected by the opening praise of the Creator hymned by the angelic choirs, or, in general, to the whole range of data pointing to such a tripartite pattern as Heinemann perceives in Jewish prayer tradition.

The great value of Giraudo's work, nonetheless, lies in the biblical roots he has demonstrated for such a bipartite structure as we see in the *Apostolic Tradition* and even earlier, perhaps, in the Strasbourg Papyrus. Indeed, while the structural significance of the three doxologies in *Didache* 10 cannot be swept aside, it is clear that there a bipartite pattern of thanksgiving and supplication is also in evidence, a pattern made still clearer in the reworking of *Didache* in *Apostolic Constitutions* VII. I believe that Giraudo has enhanced our appreciation of the dynamics of this bipartite pattern as Heineman has for the significance of the tripartite structure. From Cappadocia to Edessa by A.D. 300, eucharistic prayers celebrated in a Christian form the "triad" of which Heinemann speaks, the beginning of sacred history in Creation, the critical mid-point of this history in the Revelation of God in Christ and his inauguration of redemption, and the future of the covenant people moved by the indwelling of the Spirit toward the consummation of sacred history when redemption will be fulfilled—all of this serving as the liturgical backdrop against which theological reflection completed its articulation of our Trinitarian faith.

Elsewhere, as at Rome, a bipartite pattern perdured, its thanksgiving variable and the more or less fixed prayer, the canon, supplicatory throughout. The occurrence of the institution narrative and anamnesis within that supplicatory environment is one, but only one, of the factors to be considered in a comprehensive taxonomy of the anaphora and poses but one of the questions facing our continuing investigation of the origins and development of eucharistic prayer.

This investigation has not yielded, and may never yield, a totally satisfying picture of the several paths taken by evolution, but it has yielded some valuable correctives to misperceptions that enjoyed wide currency but a short time ago, some of which are still reiterated. Although the evidences remaining to us from the first centuries of the tradition are few in number—hardly more than stepping stones across a torrent of ignorance—patient reflection upon their relation to one another, to the prayer tradition that preceded them, and to the tradition that followed them, seems sure to give an ever richer resonance to our response to the ancient bidding: *Gratias agamus Domino.*

Notes

1. Frank Gavin, *The Jewish Antecedents of the Christian Sacraments*(London: S.P.C.K., 1928), Lecture III.

2. J.-P. Audet, "Literary Forms and Contents of a Normal *Eucharistia* in the First Century," *Studia Evangelica. Texte und Untersuchungen*, vol. 73 (1959) 643-662.

3. R. Ledogar, "The Eucharistic Prayer and the Gifts over Which It Is Spoken," *Worship* 41 (1967) 578-596; reprinted in R. Kevin Seasoltz, ed., *Living Bread, Saving Cup* (Collegeville: The Liturgical Press, 1987) 60-79. The point is more fully developed in his doctoral dissertation, *Acknowledgement: Praise Verbs in the Early Greek Anaphoras* (Rome: Herder, 1968).

4. Among many others, Karl Völker, *Mysterium und Agape* (Gotha: Leopold Klotz, 1927) 21, n. 2; Frank Gavin, *The Jewish Antecedents* 71f.; Gregory Dix, *The Shape of the Liturgy* (London: Dacre, 1945) 79.

5. L. Bouyer, *Eucharist: Theology and Spirituality of the Eucharistic Prayer* (Notre Dame: University of Notre Dame Press, 1968). Bouyer's argument became unnecesssarily convoluted by his attempt to combine the meal grace with the *Tefillah* from the synagogue service. Rather more perceptive was the important article of L. Ligier, "The Origins of the Eucharistic Prayer: From the Last Supper to the Eucharist," *Studia Liturgica* 9 (1973) 176-185. It should be noted that the fourth *berakah* found in the Grace after Meals today was introduced only in the second century of our era.

6. Thomas J. Talley, "From *Berakah* to *Eucharistia*: A Reopening Question," *Worship* 50 (1976) 115-137; reprinted in Seasoltz, *Living Bread* 80-101.

7. Joseph Heinemann, *Prayer in the Talmud: Forms and Patterns*, Studia Judaica: Forschungen zur Wissenschaft des Judentums, vol. 9 (Berlin and New York: Walter de Gruyter, 1977).

8. Ibid. 88. In my own 1975 paper, against Audet's understanding of this element as a return to the opening blessing theme, I ventured, "rather than being a purely formal return to the opening theme (such as we see in a dance movement's return to the scherzo after the trio), the *chatimah* would seem to have the function of making *berakoth* of prayers that otherwise would not be." (Seasoltz, *Living Bread* 87.)

9. James H. Charlesworth, ed., *The Old Testament Pseudepigrapha*, vol. 2 (Garden City, NY: Doubleday & Co., 1985) 97. The translation is by

O.S. Wintermute. The quotation marks in the text, of course, are an initiative of the translator not found in the Ethiopic.

10. Heinemann, *Prayer in the Talmud* 33.

11. Cf. R.C.D. Jasper and G.J. Cuming, *Prayers of the Eucharist: Early and Reformed*, 3rd rev. ed. (New York: Pueblo Publishing Co., 1987) 31-38 (the text of the prayer is on p. 35).

12. G. Garitte, "Un opuscule grec traduit de l'arménien sur l'addition d'eau au vin eucharistique," *Le Muséon* 73 (1960) 297-310. A convenient English version is found in Jasper, *Prayers* 141-142. Although the structure is relatively primitive, the theological development evident in this prayer suggests a date after the Council of Chalcedon.

13. Jasper, *Prayers* 23-24. See John W. Riggs, "From Gracious Table to Sacramental Elements: The Tradition-History of Didache 9 and 10," *The Second Century* 4:2 (1984) 83-101.

14. The bracketed words are lacking in the Coptic version and, on this ground, are omitted from the excellent reconstitution of the text by John Riggs, "From Gracious Table."

15. Talley, "From *Berakah* to *Eucharistia*" 128-129 [Seasoltz, *Living Bread* 93-94]. See Henri Cazelles, "L'Anaphore et l'ancien testament," *Eucharisties d'Orient et d'Occident*, vol. 1, Lex Orandi, vol. 36 (Paris: Editions du Cerf, 1970) 11-21; Jean Laporte, *Eucharistia in Philo*, Studies in the Bible and Early Christianity, vol. 3 (New York: E. Mellen Press, 1983).

16. Cesare Giraudo, S.J., *La struttura letteraria della preghiera eucaristica: Saggio sulla genesi letteraria di una forma*, Analecta Biblica, vol. 92 (Rome: Biblical Institute Press, 1981).

17. Louis Ligier ("The Origins of the Eucharistic Prayer" 161-185) suggested that the institution narrative and anamnesis were assigned places in either the Christological thanksgiving or the supplication for the church, following models established by festal embolisms in one or the other of these elements of the Jewish meal grace. These festal embolisms are not the same as the embolisms of which Giraudo speaks, as he makes clear (p. 242, n. 83).

18. Giraudo, *La struttura letteraria* 192.

19. Bryan D. Spinks, "The Jewish Sources for the Sanctus," *The Heythrop Journal* 21 (1980) 173.

20. C.P. Price, "Jewish Morning Prayer and Early Christian Anaphoras," *Anglican Theological Review* 43 (1961) 153-168; Jacob Vellian, "The Anaphoral Structure of *Addai and Mari* Compared to the *Berakoth* Preceding the Shema in the Synagogue Morning Service," *Le Muséon* 85 (1972) 201-223; Brian Spinks, "The Original Form of the Anaphora of the Apostles: A Suggestion in the Light of Maronite Sharar," *Ephemerides Liturgicae* 91 (1977) 146-161.

21. J. Mann, "Genizah Fragments of the Palestinian Order of Service," *Hebrew Union College Annual* 2 (1925) 289-290.

22. Heinemann, *Prayer in the Talmud* 231f.

23. Hansjörg Auf der Maur, *Die Osterhomilien des Asterios Sophistes als Quelle für die Geschichte der Osterfeier*, Trierer theologische Studien, vol. 19 (Trier: Paulinus Verlag, 1967) 74-94.

24. Since this chapter was originally written, the prayers of the *Apostolic Constitutions* have received the meticulous study that they have long deserved. See David Fiensy, *Prayers Alleged to be Jewish: An Examination of the Constitutiones Apostolorum*, Brown Judaic Studies vol. 65 (Chico, CA: Scholars Press, 1985). He argues convincingly that the prayers in Book VII.33-38 represent Christian adaptations of a synagogue service for the Sabbath morning.

25. William Macomber, "The Ancient Form of the *Anaphora of the Apostles*," *East of Byzantium: Syria and Armenia in the Formative Period*, Dumbarton Oaks Symposium, 1980 (Washington, D.C., 1982) 73-88. Macomber had made this suggestion tentatively in "The Maronite and Chaldean Versions of the Anaphora of the Apostles," *Orientalia Christiana Periodica* 37 (1971) 58-66, an essay to which Giraudo refers without taking note of Macomber's suggestion.

26. The opening prayer, like the *berakoth*, begins, "Praise to *thee*," but thereafter uses only third person pronouns, "who created the world in his goodness," etc. The translation of Spinks (cf. the following note) places these in the second person as is customary in translation.

27. Quoted here from the excellent edition of Bryan Spinks, *Addai and Mari—The Anaphora of the Apostles: A Text for Students*, Grove Liturgical Study No. 24 (Bramcote, Notts, 1980) 17. Cf. Jasper, *Prayers* 47. Macomber renders it, "We too, Lord, thy sinful servants give thee thanks . . ." In note 8 he observes that the absence of a transitional phrase of Addai and Mari at this point, "With these heavenly hosts, we give thanks," has been taken by some as evidence that the prayer once lacked the *Sanctus*. Against this argument he insists that the prayer begins "We *too*, Lord . . .," making the same connection to the preceding *Sanctus*. The usual Syriac word for "too" or "also"—*ap*—is not employed, but the intensification of the first person plural verb with the personal pronoun can suggest his translation. However, in a personal communication, Macomber graciously conceded that such a reading as that of Spinks is equally possible.

28. He presents, e.g., the text of Addai and Mari without taking any note of the structure indicated by rubrics in the mss. In Giraudo's presentation of the text, there are but two sections, anamnetic and epicletic, the former comprised of the first two sections in the critical text on which he bases his version. The rubrical title for the *qanona* that

concludes the first *gehanta*, i.e., the *Sanctus*, while it appears in the Mar Eshaya ms., is omitted in Giraudo's text and the *Sanctus* thus appears in the middle of the first part of Giraudo's text with no argument for this restructuring of the prayer.

29. Thomas J. Talley, "The Literary Structure of the Eucharistic Prayer," *Worship* 58 (1984) 413.

30. Cf. note 11 above.

31. H. Engberding, "Zur griechischen Epiphaniusliturgie," *Le Muséon* 74 (1961) 135-142. The Anaphora of Timotheus has been edited by Adolphus Rücher in A. Raes, *Anaphorae Syriacae*, vol. 1 (Rome, 1939) 9-47, and his Latin version is reproduced in Anton Hänggi and Irmgard Pahl, *Prex Eucharistica*, Spicilegium Friburgense, vol. 12 (Fribourg Suisse: Editions Universitaires, 1968) 276-280.

32. Jasper, *Prayers* 67-73. The editors assert (p. 67): "It may well be dated to the late third century."

33. On this "double epiklesis" and its relation to the tradition, see Aidan Kavanagh, "Thoughts on the New Eucharistic Prayers," in Seasoltz, *Living Bread* 102-112; Richard Albertine, "The Problem of the (Double) Epiklesis in the New Roman Eucharistic Prayers," *Ephemerides Liturgicae* 91 (1977) 193-202; Enrico Mazza, *The Eucharistic Prayers of the Roman Rite* (New York: Pueblo Publishing Co., 1986) 92.

34. Another fragment representing a local use, formerly at Louvain (Coptica 27) but no longer extant, follows the *Sanctus* with an anamnesis, oblation, and consecratory epiklesis, all prior to the institution narrative. The Greek original of this evidently fourth century anaphora has been recognized in a papyrus at Barcelona.

35. Jasper, *Prayers* 53-54.

36. Edward Kilmartin, "Sacrificium Laudis," *Theological Studies* 35 (1974) 268-287.

37. Geoffrey Cuming, "The Anaphora of St. Mark: A Study in Development," *Le Muséon* 95 (1982) 115-129. Cuming reiterated his views regarding the Strasbourg papyrus at the Ninth Oxford Patristic Conference in a short communication published in *Worship* 58 (1984) 168-172. Bryan Spinks, "A Complete Anaphora? A Note on Strasbourg Gr. 254," *The Heythrop Journal* 25 (1984) 51-55 has taken issue with all the arguments for the integrity of Stras. 254, but his argument deals primarily with these authors' attempts to treat the text as related to the Jewish *berakah* form. In fact, evidence for a Jewish parentage is so slight as to be imperceptible in this instance, it seems to me, and treatment of the papyrus' doxology as a *chatimah* is imprecise at best. That *Didache* 10 has doxologies where *Birkat Ha-Mazon* had *chatimoth* does not allow us to see every doxology as a *chatimah*.

38. Herman Wegman, "Une anaphore incomplète? Les Fragments sur

Papyrus Strasbourg Gr. 254," in *Studies in Gnosticism and Hellenistic Religions*, eds., R. van den Broek and M.J. Vermaseren (Leiden: Brill, 1981) 432-450.

39. W.H. Bates, "Thanksgiving and Intercession in the Liturgy of St. Mark," in *The Sacrifice of Praise*, ed. by Bryan D. Spinks, Bibliotheca "Ephemerides Liturgicae," "Subsidia" vol. 19 (Rome, 1981) 118f.

40. Jasper, *Prayers* 53-54.

41. This is clear in the Mar Saba fragment now included in Ursula Treu's 1980 second edition of Otto Stälin, *Clemens Alexandrinus*, vol. 4, part 1 (Die griechischen christlichen Schriftsteller der ersten Jahrhunderte) xvii-xviii. The attribution of this letter to Clement, however, is not unchallenged.

42. Hans Bernard Meyer, "Das Werden der literarischen Strucktur des Hochgebetes," *Zeitschrift für katholische Theologie* 105.2 (1983) 201; Albert Gerhards, "Die literarische Strucktur des eucharistischen Hochgebets," *Liturgisches Jahrbuch* 33 (1983) 90-104.

43. P. 266 and n. 158.

44. Gerhards, "Die literarische Strucktur." The reference is to H. Gese, "Die Herkunft des Herrenmahls," in his *Zur biblischen Theologie, Alttestamentliche Vorträge* (Munich, 1977) 107-127 [E.T.=*Essays on Biblical Theology*, Keith Grim, trans. (Minneapolis: Augsburg, 1981).

3

The Windsor Statement
and the Eucharistic Prayer

SINCE THE SECOND VATICAN COUNCIL THE WHOLE OF THE CHRISTIAN
Church has been enriched by a complex web of ecumenical discussions between major traditions, a significant furthering of the
important ecumenical work of the Faith and Order Movement
prior to the council. These post-conciliar consultations between
particular traditions have in many cases revealed the extent to
which past polarizations have been overcome by subsequent
theological development. A case in point is the notable progress
made by the discussions between Anglicans and Roman Cath-
olics, discussions whose first important fruit was the Agreed
Statement on Eucharistic Doctrine issued at the commission's
third meeting at Windsor, 7 September 1971. This statement, the
result of two years of deliberation, seeks to articulate, as the
co-chairmen's preface says, "the Christian faith of the Eucharist."[1]

Given the history of the polemic between our churches regarding the eucharist, that a statement on "the Christian faith of the
Eucharist" could be agreed upon is testimony to the patience,
persistence, and insight of the theologians on the commission.
That their energies were so employed, however, is surely testimony to the operation of the Holy Spirit in the church in our time,
and it is testimony as well to the fresh access of the spirit to our
hardened heads and hearts in and following the Second Vatican
Council.

Post-Conciliar Eucharistic Prayers

The first of the documents of this council, rightly characterized by J.M.R. Tillard as among the more important documents of Christian history,[2] is the Constitution on the Sacred Liturgy, *Sacrosanctum Concilium*. This document provides the fundamental theology of worship in general and of the eucharist in particular that can be recognized at point after point of the Windsor Agreed Statement. The constitution also calls for a general revision of the liturgical rites of the Roman Catholic Church, including the eucharist, and this work of revision has proved as important for other western churches as it has for the Roman Catholic, since this initiative of liturgical revision revitalized similar initiatives already at work in other churches and at many points stimulated those other enterprises along the same lines as those taken by the Concilium for the Implementation of the Constitution on the Liturgy. In one particular matter, the Anglican Churches seem to have pursued enthusiastically a novel initiative of the Roman Concilium, the provision of a number of eucharistic prayers from which the celebrant of the eucharist might choose, this by contrast to the single canon or "prayer of consecration" which had, in spite of small changes, been characteristic of both our churches for centuries.

The sixteenth century, of course, saw this prayer changed in England, but that done, it remained the one and only such prayer. A different eucharistic prayer was adopted by the Episcopal Church in this country in its first *Book of Common Prayer* in 1789, but this, too, remained as fixed and invariable as the Roman Canon.

Today, by contrast, the Roman Missal provides four complete eucharistic prayers, with still others authorized for Masses of Reconciliation or Masses for Children. The Alternative Service Book of the Church of England provides six new eucharistic prayers, and the American *Book of Common Prayer*, although retaining that which we first adoped in 1789, adds five new ones, plus two other forms in which a fixed nucleus allows for flexibility in the content of praise and thanksgiving and intercessory commemorations within the eucharistic prayer. Similar developments have occurred in other Anglican provinces.[3]

Such a rash of new eucharistic prayers is a liturgical phenomenon hardly observed since the patristic age. As such, they offer an important opportunity, I believe, to illuminate the Agreed Statement on Eucharistic Doctrine, to test its limits, and perhaps to suggest some directions in future ecumenical discussion of the eucharist.

The Agreed Statement makes two references to the eucharistic prayer, the first in the context of its discussion of "The eucharist and the sacrifice of Christ," and the second in the following section on "The presence of Christ." The first reference (toward the end of paragraph 5) says:

> In the eucharistic prayer the Church continues to make a perpetual memorial of Christ's death, and his members, united with God and one another, give thanks for all his mercies, entreat the benefits of his passion on behalf of the whole church, participate in the benefits and enter into the movement of his self-offering.[4]

The second reference is in paragraph 10 and is more focused on the consecratory dimension of the eucharistic mystery. It says:

> According to the traditional order of the liturgy the consecratory prayer (*anaphora*) leads to the communion of the faithful. Through this prayer of thanksgiving, a word of faith addressed to the Father, the bread and wine become the body and blood of Christ by the action of the Holy Spirit, so that in communion we eat the flesh of Christ and drink his blood.[5]

Neither of these texts comments in any detail on the structure of the eucharistic prayer, and this is understandable, given the variety in such structures. In one particular, however, it would be helpful to know how, in the eucharistic prayers themselves, the two elements discussed here—the memorial offering of Christ's passion and the consecration of his body and blood—are understood to relate to one another.

Relation between Offering and Consecration

It has been found helpful in modern discussions to avoid too great specificity in identifying the precise point of the eucharistic consecration. The entire prayer, it is frequently said today, is consecratory. And, one may assume, the same can be said of the offering dimension of the eucharist. The prayer is regularly called, as our document notes, *anaphora*, "the offering." One might then suppose that the entire prayer is a prayer of oblation. This, however, does not allow any clear understanding of the relation between these two dimensions of the eucharist. Our document has gone very far indeed in reflecting the degree of our recovery from the doctrinal excesses on either side in the sixteenth century. Yet the new eucharistic prayers do not always seem to manifest that same unanimity. This is particularly true as concerns the relationship between the eucharistic sacrifice and the consecration of the eucharistic elements.

Only a few years before Vatican II, in 1960 in fact, Francis Clark, responding to C.W. Dugmore, was able to show that the more regrettable destruction theories of eucharistic sacrifice, theories of the eucharist which saw there a sacrament of Christ's destruction—expressed sometimes as the humiliation of reduction to the appearances of bread and wine, sometimes as the separation of his blood from his body through their separate consecration—such destruction theories, Clark showed, were post-Tridentine phenomena and played no part in the Reformation polemic. Yet Clark himself, seeking to set forth the more sane, balanced, and (to him) plainly traditional teaching of medieval theologians, urges that in their teaching the eucharist was a sacrifice in four senses: (a) the sacrifice of praise and thanksgiving; (b) the memorial of Christ's self-oblation on Calvary; (c) the oblation of ourselves; and (d) the offering of Christ's body and blood. Clark thus seeks to demonstrate the purity of Catholic teaching and the culpability of Protestant deviations from it. He characterizes the English reformers as "waging an intensive campaign against the belief that the Christian priesthood is essentially ordained to bring about the real presence of Christ by the Eucharistic consecration and to offer him thus objectively present in a propitiatory sacrifice for the living and dead."[6] He seems not to recognize that there was or could be a question about the treatment of the sacramental body and blood of Christ as sacrificial victim within the mainstream of Catholic tradition.

In fact, this understanding of the relation of the eucharistic presence to the eucharistic sacrifice, although probably common teaching in the late Middle Ages, would be difficult to find stated in just such terms prior to the *Canonis Missae Expositio* of Gabriel Biel, the first professor of theology at Tübingen in the fifteenth century.[7] In his exposition, Biel made it clear that in the anamnesis of the Canon Missae (the paragraph following the institution narrative, which begins *Unde et memores*) the body and blood of Christ are offered to the Father, having just been made present through the recitation of the institution narrative immediately preceding.

Two centuries earlier, Thomas Aquinas also understood the narrative of the institution to be focus of the consecration of the eucharist. However, he situated the sacrificial aspect of the eucharist prior to the consecration. In *Summa Theologiae* III.83.4, Thomas decribes the structure of the Mass, explaining the preparatory character of the entrance rite and the instruction afforded by the scripture reading. He then continues:

> So then, after the people have been prepared and instructed, the next step is to proceed to the celebration of the mystery, which is both offered as a sacrifice, and consecrated and received as a sacrament: since first we have the oblation; then the consecration of the matter offered; and thirdly, its reception.

This offering of the oblation, he makes clear, is what we know as the offertory, the texts consisting of the offertory chant and the variable *oratio super oblata*. He makes no reference to the complex of sacrificial prayers by the celebrant that were, at least by the sixteenth century, known as the "little canon," and it seems altogether likely that these were in fact absent from the Dominican rite of his day. This identification of the offertory action as the sacrificial oblation, of course, leaves the canon a purely consecratory prayer, and one might well wonder what he made of *Unde et memores*, the anamnesis following the institution narrative, which offers the gifts of bread and wine as memorial of Christ's death and resurrection. It is this anamnesis that is the focus of oblation in virtually all the early eucharistic prayers from the *Apostolic Tradition* forward. Not so for Thomas, in spite of the text's unequivocal *offerimus*. Rather, having described the consecration by the words of Christ, Thomas says:

> Thirdly, he makes excuse for his presumption in obeying
> Christ's command, saying: Wherefore, calling to mind, etc.
> [i.e., *Unde et memores.*]

Given the Angelic Doctor's acceptance of the consecratory effect of the *verba Christi*, it is not difficult to understand his diffidence toward expounding the clear meaning of that anamnesis.
It would lead, he seems to have recognized, to exactly the position taken later by Biel, that the priest offers to the Father the
body and blood of Christ, a view which seems to have been no
more acceptable to Aquinas than it would be to the reformers.

Oblation in Eucharistic Prayer IV

The later opinion of Biel has perdured to a considerable extent,
as can be seen in the matter cited from Francis Clark. Indeed, this
point of view finally achieved overt liturgical expression in Eucharistic Prayer IV of the Missal of Paul VI. This prayer was
broadly inspired by the Alexandrian version of the anaphora of
St. Basil of Caesarea, but the Roman conviction of the consecratory efficacy of the words of Christ at the institution made a
consecratory epiklesis after that point, such an epiklesis as we see
in the Anaphora of Basil, quite impossible since it would imply
that the consecration had not already been accomplished. Therefore, in the Roman version of that prayer, as in all the new
eucharistic prayers, there is an epiklesis prior to the institution
narrative that invokes the Holy Spirit for the consecration of the
gifts. Then the anamnesis which follows the institution narrative in Prayer IV speaks with a rather inexorable logic when it
prays:

> Father, we now celebrate this memorial of our redemption.
> We recall Christ's death, his descent among the dead, his
> resurrection, and his ascension to your right hand; and, look-
> ing forward to his coming in glory, we offer you his body
> and blood, the acceptable sacrifice which brings salvation to
> the whole world.

This view of the content of the eucharistic sacrifice is no novelty to the tradition of manual theology, having been repeated

with fair regularity since Biel, but it is new to liturgical expression, in spite of the Concilium's assurance that "these new texts possess a most definitely traditional character." One might well remember here once again the trenchant comment of the eminent Benedictine scholar, Professor Aidan Kavanagh, on the anamnesis of Prayer IV:

> This is novel, and can hardly be said to retain "a most definitely traditional character." One who has some acquaintance with the medieval and reformation history of eucharistic controversy will recognize the inadequacy of such a position, and may be forgiven his disappointment that its tendentiousness has got into a Catholic formulary precisely at a time when it could have been diagnosed and avoided most easily.[8]

In the same volume of *Worship* as that in which Professor Kavanagh comments on the new eucharistic prayers, Dr. John Jay Hughes correctly pointed to the sound doctrine of justification still to be seen in the Canon Missae, in spite of the theological commentary and the works piety that confronted Luther.[9] And he is not alone in rejecting the theological interpretation of Biel and much of the tradition following him. He cites, for example, in his own translation from the German of *Missarum Solemnia*, these words of the deeply conservative Joseph Jungmann:

> It is therefore at least highly improbable that, as most interpreters declare, only the consecrated gifts as such are meant by the *de tuis donis ac datis* of the prayer *Unde et memores*.[10]

Hughes further quotes Jungmann's Jesuit successor at Innsbruck, Fr. Hans Bernard Meyer, as saying that the oblationary language after the institution narrative

> does not say that we take the divine-human person of Jesus Christ in our hands, as it were, in order to offer him to the Father. Rather, they speak of our gifts, of the bread and the cup, and of our offering; and what we offer is the gifts which we can apprehend with our senses.[11]

Meyer's statement continues with a point which I believe to be critical for any attempt at theological commentary on the eucharist, including perhaps especially any attempt at an ecumenical consensus.

> Moreover we are dealing in the canon not with dogmatic definitions formulated in theological terminology, but with liturgical prayers. Such texts follow totally different stylistic and terminological laws which can be understood only by those who are familiar with the intellectual and liturgical climate in which these texts originated.

Oblation Oriented toward Consecration

This has been the principal concern of still another Roman Catholic commentator on ecumenical rapprochement regarding the eucharist, Father Hans-Joachim Schulz, especially in his small but uncommonly rich *Oekumenische Glaubenseinheit aus eucharistischer Ueberlieferung* (Paderborn, 1976), and more recently in a paper read before the *Societas Liturgica* in Vienna.[12] There, having cited Melancthon's acceptance of the sacrificial language of the Byzantine anaphora, he argued, as he had in his earlier work, that the tradition of the eucharistic prayer from the *Apostolic Tradition* through the entire Syro-Byzantine tradition, and for much of that history and still today in Coptic tradition as well, it is only after the anamnesis, the memorial of the death and resurrection of the Lord made in the thank-offering of our gifts of bread and wine, that the church has prayed for the outpouring of the Spirit upon us and those gifts to make them the body and the blood of the Lord for our union with him and with one another in him. Holy communion and the eucharistic consecration which enables it are the *consequence* of our anamnesis of Christ's unique act of self-oblation at the center of salvation history, a memorial accomplished in our thankful oblation of ourselves expressed in the oblations of bread and wine, so that by the Holy Spirit they and we may be filled with his life.

Such had been much earlier the viewpoint of Monsignor Louis Duchesne who, following Nicholas Cabasilas,[13] saw the Roman Canon's equivalent of the oriental invocation of the Spirit after the anamnesis in *Supplices te rogamus*, the prayer that the gifts be carried by the hands of the angel to the heavenly altar, noting that it is only from that point on that they are spoken of as Christ's body and blood.[14] This would afford an interpretation of the Canon Missae consistent with the Byzantine, West Syrian, and Coptic anaphoras, all of which are, we must remember, in regular use within the non-Latin rites of the Roman Catholic Church. It is, then, with particular gratitude that one takes note of the publication and distribution for study of a careful edition of the eucharistic prayer of the *Apostolic Tradition* of Hippolytus by the Roman Catholic International Commission on English in the Liturgy, and their projected issuance, again for study, of further eucharistic prayers in which the invocation of the Holy Spirit for the consecration of the gifts is united with the invocation of the Spirit upon the communicants and follows after the institution narrative and the memorial oblation, suggesting the same relationship between oblation and consecration as was urged by Thomas Aquinas, "first we have the oblation; then the consecration of the matter offered; and thirdly, its reception."

By contrast to this order, in the Church of England's Alternative Service Book, as in the Missal of Paul VI, every eucharistic prayer boasts an invocation of the Holy Spirit for the consecration of the gifts prior to the institution of the Holy Spirit for the consecration of the gifts prior to the institition narrative, a feature already of Cranmer's rewriting of *Quam oblationem* in 1549, its force radically reduced from 1552 to 1662. This, of course, carries forward the general Reformation tendency to treat the scriptural institution narrative as possessed of a divine authority that could not be accorded to the liturgical text in which it was embedded, although we may suspect as well that the reformers encountered at that point the limit of their ability to renounce the presuppositions of medieval eucharistic interpretation.

Novelty in Search of Roots

The new arrangement placing a consecratory epiklesis prior to the institution narrative and a second epiklesis on the communicants following the anamnesis has claimed roots in Egyptian tradition, but many responsible scholars have shown the vanity of this quest for precedent in the tradition. It has been common to speak of the connecting text from the *Sanctus* to the institution narrative in such anaphoras as those of Serapion and St. Mark as an epiklesis, but these transitional passages cannot be confused with the explicity consecratory epikleses following the institution narrative and anamnesis in these prayers. As noted previously, one late (500-700) fragment from a monastery in Upper Egypt, Dêr Balyzeh, does situate its consecratory epiklesis before the institution narrative, but the fragment breaks off before it can afford any information regarding either oblation in the anamnesis or a second epiklesis.[15] Another evidence of an Egyptian local use, a Coptic papyrus formerly at Louvain, places immediately following the *Sanctus* both the anamnesis and oblation and the invocation of the Holy Spirit for the consecration.

> Heaven and earth are full of that glory wherewith you glorified us through your only-begotten Son Jesus Christ, the first-born of all creation, sitting at the right hand of your majesty in heaven, who will come to judge the living and the dead. We make the remembrance of his death, offering to you your creatures, this bread and this cup. We pray and beseech you to send out over them your Holy Spirit, the Paraclete, from heaven . . . to make (?) the bread the body of Christ and the cup the blood of Christ of the new covenant.[16]

The institution narrative follows. Here the usual order is retained, the anamnesis with its oblation leading into the epiklesis for the consecration of the gifts. Here too, then, there is no basis for a consecratory invocation of the Spirit preceding the anamnesis with its oblation.

The novel liturgical structure setting the consecratory epiklesis prior to the institution narrative and anamnesis has the effect of assuring the association of the consecration of the eucharist with the institution narrative, however much liturgists may insist that it is the entire anaphora that effects consecration. The result of this continuing association of consecration with the institution narrative is that any oblation following this narrative must choose between Biel's understanding of the eucharistic sacrifice or prescind from the matter entirely as far as the eucharistic gifts are concerned. Given this painfully limited choice, it is not surprising that we encounter no overt oblation of the gifts in any anamnesis of the eucharistic prayers of The Alternative Service

Book, nor is it surprising that the Windsor statement on the eucharist displays such diffidence in grasping the nettle of eucharistic sacrifice, a theme that has always loomed large in eucharistic prayer and theology, and has been at the heart of controversy between and within our two traditions.

This diffidence, of course, is not to be despised. It is, nonetheless, to be transcended, by God's own wisdom in God's own time. Until then, the limited success of the Agreed Statement may serve to remind us that Prosper of Aquitaine really did say *legem credendi lex statuat supplicandi*, not simply *lex orandi, lex credendi*. In matters concerning the sacramental mysteries, rite and its prayer are primary. The Reformation of the sixteenth century taught us as dramatically as could be wished that theological preconception is no basis for the reconstruction *ex nihilo* of the church's liturgical prayer. Four centuries and more have seen the eucharist itself teach us how better to pray. If we can risk attending to the tradition of the prayer itself and allow theology to flow from it, there seems every reason to hope that the achievement of the Agreed Statement on the Eucharist will soon seem but a first glimpse at the unity to which we are called, the unity which the creative Word has decreed, and in which we must learn to live.

Notes

1. Anglican-Roman Catholic International Commission, *The Final Report* (Washington, D.C.: U.S. Catholic Conference; Cincinnati: Forward Movement Publications, 1982) 11.

2. A remark of Father Tillard in an earlier paper at the same colloquium at which this paper was originally presented.

3. I beg forgiveness of my fellow Anglicans in Australia, Canada, Scotland, and other parts, for my failure to report on the progress of their own liturgical reforms, and mention only the United States and England simply to illustrate the phenomenon.

4. *The Final Report* 14.

5. Ibid. 15-16.

6. Francis Clark, S.J., *Eucharistic Sacrifice and the Reformation* (Westminster, MD: Newman Press; London: Darton, Longman, & Todd, 1960) 191.

7. Gabriel Biel, *Canonis missae expositio*, ed., Heiko A. Oberman and Wm. J. Courtney (Wiesbaden: Franz Steiner Verlag, 1965) Part 2, Lect. 54. Vol. 1, pp. 335-344 (cf. especially pp. 340-342).

8. Aidan Kavanagh, "Thoughts on the New Eucharistic Prayers," *Worship* 43 (1969). [Reprinted in R. Kevin Seasoltz, ed., *Living Bread,Saving Cup: Readings on the Eucharist* (Collegeville: The Liturgical Press, 1987) 109.]

9. John Jay Hughes, "Eucharistic Sacrifice: Transcending the Reformation Deadlock," *Worship* 43 (1969) 532-544.

10. Ibid. 539, n. 17.

11. Ibid. 539. The reference is to Hans Bernard Meyer, *Luther und die Messe* (1965) 251-252.

12. Hans-Joachim Schulz, "Patterns of Offering and Sacrifice," *Studia Liturgica* 15 (1982-83) 34-48.

13. Nicholas Cabasilas, *A Commentary on the Divine Liturgy*, chapter 30. A convenient translation is that of J.M. Hussey and P.A. McNulty, published by St. Vladimir's Seminary Press (Crestwood, NY, 1977) 76-79.

14. Louis Duchesne, *Christian Worship: Its Origin and Evolution* (London: S.P.C.K., 1956) 181-182.

15. R.C.D. Jasper and G.C. Cuming, *Prayers of the Eucharist: Early and Reformed*, 3rd ed. (New York: Pueblo Publishing Co., 1987) 79-81.

16. Ibid. 81. This papyrus fragment, published with a Greek retroversion by Th. Lefort, "Coptica lovanensia," *Le Muséon* 53 (1940) 22-24, no. 27, but now destroyed by fire, was of the sixth century. Cuming reports that the Greek original of this prayer has been identified in a presently unpublished papyrus at Barcelona, written in the fourth century.

4

Healing: Sacrament or Charism?

PARAGRAPH 6 OF THE INTRODUCTION TO THE DRAFT REVISION OF THE Roman Catholic rites for the sick, in speaking of the effects of the sacrament of anointing, sets before us the concern of this chapter. "The proper grace of this sacrament gives strength to the sick person. This grace endows him with God-given peace of soul to bear his suffering. It also effects the forgiveness of his sins, if this is necessary. And, if God so wills, the sacramental anointing can even effect a total restoration of physical health."[1]

The last mentioned effect, "a total restoration of physical health," reflects a significant shift of nuance from the parallel statement of Trent. Whereas the first schema of that council's decree on the sacrament of extreme unction would have limited the administration of the anointing "only to those who are in their final struggle and who have come to grips with death and who are about to go forth to the Lord,"[2] chapter 2 of the final version says of the effects of the anointing:

> This reality is the grace of the Holy Spirit, whose anointing wipes away sins, provided there are still some to be expiated, as well as the remnants of sin, and comforts and strengthens the soul of the sick person, by arousing in him great confidence in the divine mercy; encouraged thereby, the sick person bears more easily the difficulties and trials of his illness, and resists more readily the temptations of the demon *who lies in wait for the heel* [Gn 3:15], and where it is

47

> expedient for the health of the soul, he receives, at times, health of body.[3]

Here, the gift of bodily health is looked upon as ancillary to the good of the soul, while the more recent statement seems to suggest that the total restoration of physical health is a more ultimate good toward which the other effects of the sacrament tend.

In both statements, however, it is clear that physical healing remains a matter of some uncertainty. This may be forthcoming if God so wills it, but the sacrament itself gives no assurance that healing will be the outcome. In such a case, then, one may well wonder in what sense physical healing can be considered an *effect* of the sacrament. If healing occurs, is such a restoration of bodily health a proper consequence of the sacrament, or has the will of God responded to some well-intentioned but nonsacramental prayer of the patient or the intercession of the church, or has God even willed the restoration of health without reference to any of these things? Or again, to consider all the possibilities, does the will of God at times operate even within and through certain of the arcane procedures of what we call "medical science"?

The point of all such haggling is not merely to cavil at the Tridentine anathemas, but to pose the more serious question of the cause/effect model in the theological articulation of the sacraments, a habit of medieval theological method that is thrown into high relief by this question, a habit that reduces the many-layered and richly textured liturgical experience of the church to a moment narrowly defined as the production of an effect in the recipient. This effect is usually cast up in theological terms, which defy empirical verification. The case before us, however, first suggests healing to be a verifiable effect, and then seeks to weasel out on that by acknowledging that we are here before the incomprehensible mystery of the divine will—while continuing to assert that one of the possible outcomes, should it occur, will also be an effect of the sacrament. And what is left to one side is serious address to the liturgical phenomenon itself, to its sociological and psychological dimensions, its relation to the whole sacramental economy, to a theology of the liturgy in general, to ecclesiology, to soteriology, to eschatology, and to theology.

Sacramental Efficacy

That such a diatribe as this is unfair does not amount to saying that it is whipping a dead horse. Probably no sacramental theology has ever been quite so narrow as the above critique would suggest, but it remains true that as consideration of the sacrament of anointing has sought to treat this rite as something more than a final perfection of penance *in extremis*, there has come an increasing blurring of the distinction between the church's liturgical address to affliction and the charism of thaumaturgy, the effecting of miraculous cures, and with that blurring of distinction, a serious confusion regarding the whole nature of sacramental realities. Just as we have learned once again to discern the profound ecclesiological dimensions of baptism and eucharist, as we have passed beyond limiting baptism to removal of the guilt of original sin and can see eucharist as a bit more than a dole of divinity to a dissociated communicant, we seem, in the case of the anointing of the sick, to be driven further toward a preoccupation with the effect on the individual recipient, a preoccupation which is all the more problematic when emphasis falls on restoration of bodily health, for this brings to a situation already laden with anxiety a well-nigh inescapable tendency to administer the rite and then stand back and see if it is going to work.

Even allowing for wide variation in the quality of rites and the manner of their celebration, we need to remind ourselves that sacraments always "work," and therefore what is claimed for them must be articulated within that certainty. That is to say, sacramental and liturgical realities are always and only that, and we do the theology of the liturgy no service by extravagant claims of extrinsic effects. Too many communities have already been brought to despair by the discovery that, having rearranged the furniture of the sanctuary and instituted an offertory procession, they still don't love one another. And, though one is ashamed to say it, there are those who have been told that sacraments and prayer in true faith would remove a malignant tumor, and so have learned from its continued growth the insufficiency of their faith, and have died in despair. And this because liturgy was confounded with charism.

The claims for healing in the Roman Catholic documents cited are mild indeed, but one can detect the beginning of a trend toward a preoccupation with physical healing such as has grown very rapidly in the Anglican Communion without the benefit of serious theological criticism, and has begun to assert that sickness and suffering are unqualifiedly contrary to the will of God. One does not need to go deeply into a Teilhardian view of the interrelation of life and death, of growth and decay, to suspect that such an oversimplification of the divine will as would set God always on the side of good health—that keystone of bourgeois beatitude—falls tragically short of an adequate understanding of the paschal mystery or perception of the strangeness of our salvation. The passion of Christ, his agony and death, was not a divine *lapsus* nor was it a defeat of God's holy will. Rather, the holiness of the divine will, the utter otherness of God's will, is revealed in the agony and bloody sweat, the cross and passion, the precious death and burial, as much as by Christ's mighty resurrection and glorious ascension.

On the other hand, we must never lose sight of the mystery, indeed the miracle, of healing. The body's thrust to life, its struggle against disease and decay, is indeed an expression of the primacy of life and its ultimate victory over death, a victory archetypically achieved in the resurrection of the Lord. Thus all healing can be seen as an act of God, in that no therapeutic measure can have its effect apart from the dynamism of life itself. The practice of medicine is a dialogue with the life processes, not the simple manipulation of an inert material. And at the root of this life process there still resides the profound regenerative mystery which sustains the patient, and the physician as well, in humility and hope. There is no healing that is not an act of God.

Healing as Charism

In my experience, such a broad theological principle, however, does not really speak to the concern of those most interested in spiritual healing. What is seen as important from the charismatic point of view is not merely the primary causality of God in every aspect of life or of existence, but the significant occasion in which healing seems totally out of proportion to the therapeutic measures undertaken or any reasonable hope for their success. Here there seems to be evidence of a special divine intervention at the level of secondary causality, a divine action not merely fundamental and prior to, but along side and in addition to the natural recuperative powers of the body and the potency of the therapeutic processes employed.

It is presently irrelevant that such divine intervention is most evident to those possessed of faith or disposed to it, since the question before us is not an apologetic one. Nor is it to the point that Christians, including theologians, find themselves variously impressed (or unimpressed) by such phenomena. What is more to the point is that such intervention is not covenanted, nor is it patient of liturgical institutionalization. It is, by the nature of the case under consideration, the exception to every pattern, truly a wonder, a miracle. The perception of such intervention points to the radical contingency of human life and understanding before the transcendent freedom of God, and the phenomenon is for that reason various in its manifestation and in its attendant circumstances. So Calvin, writing against the sacrament of anointing, will argue that contrary to the claims made for biblical warrant, Christ himself heals in one instance by making clay of spittle and anointing the blind man, in another by a touch, in other instances by no action at all. He argues with equal vigor, though with considerably less force, that the age of such miracles is over, and that Christians should not presume to such apostolic power.[4]

The fact would seem to be that Christians have claimed to exercise such healing power in most ages of the church, though the fashion in such charisms has been inconstant. Still, there can be no question of the claim of the charism of healing well past the apostolic age. The thaumaturge is certainly no stranger to Christian hagiography. What is to the point, it would seem, is that the thaumaturge is a stranger to the liturgical tradition. While the *Apostolic Tradition* of Hippolytus, for example, does provide for the episcopal blessing of oil to be used by the faithful in illness, it further denies the appropriateness of ordination to those who claim the gift of healing, observing that their actions themselves will speak for them.[5] The distinction would seem an important one. In Holy Orders, as in rites of initiation, the church confers roles within the community of faith, stations within the liturgical assembly; and the authorities and prerogatives involved pertain in the first instance to the faith community and its sacramental structures, to its participation in and celebration of the paschal mystery. Charisms such as healing and prophecy, while they may be found in those who are ordained, cannot be restricted to them, nor (for good or ill) can it be shown that any rite of ordination confers them.

Yet, in that passage of the Epistle of James (5:14-15) which has served as *Grundtext* for the sacrament of unction, it is precisely the presbyterate that is to be summoned when Christians fall ill, to anoint them and pray, so that the Lord may raise them up and forgive their sins. It should be noted that the early church seems to have received a different message from this text than did later generations. Its first known use by any Christian writer is its quotation in a discussion of penance by Origen.[6] Oil seems to have been regularly blessed for use by the faithful, as were foodstuffs. Oil would have been the mainstay of the domestic pharmacopoeia, and was blessed as such. But to summon the presbyters of the church to administer it does not seem to have been a concern of the early church at all. Never, indeed, has such a direct scriptural warrant been so extravagantly ignored. Our surprise at this might be mitigated somewhat by the observation that this text from James stands alone in suggesting a ritual, sacramental, liturgical role for the presbyterate in the first century. Otherwise, references to the presbyterate can suggest something much more like the administrative and adjudicatory role of the presbyterate in Jewish communities, a role which stood in some contrast to the liturgical roles of the *archesynagogos* and *chazzan* in the synagogue. Certainly, if the function of the presbyters at the sickbed was understood to be sacerdotal, it becomes difficult to understand the vast silence of eight to nine centuries on the subject apart from the questioned text itself.[7] What alternative understanding can be offered? Simply that the sickness or dying of a Christian needs above all to be held within the community, and that the presbyters are summoned as the constitutive representatives of the community, not as *thaumatourgoi*, nor even as *sacerdotes*. Their function is not to heal nor is it yet to administer last rites, but to protect the sick member from dereliction and separation from the ecclesial body.

Sickness and Sin

It would seem that it is this which best takes account of the persistent association of the rite of anointing with penitential themes, for sickness and sin go hand in hand as two modalities of disorder. Little has been so wrong-headed in pastoral theology as the reaction against the view that sickness is correlative to sin. When this meant that sickness was sent upon individuals in punishment for some specific wrongdoing on their own part, then certainly a severe reaction was needed. But the particular reaction we have offered, that is, a simple denial of any connection between the two, amounts to little more than a secularization or profanation of sickness, a denial of its profound spiritual significance. The reason for this was, perhaps, laudable enough. Given our punitive attitude toward sin, it was indeed false and cruel to contribute further to the agonies of the sick. But that punitive attitude to sin was the last thing we were prepared to call into question, and that in turn because we could not see beyond an understanding of sin as the misdeed of an individual.

We are learning better now, it would seem. We no longer suppose as glibly as we once did that disorder can be divided into guilty and innocent. Rather, we engage disorder as agents and as patients, and usually as both. In either case, the person in disorder is out of order. There is for the individual a *de facto* rupture of communion with society and the cosmos. In sickness, one's place in the world is stripped of its grace, and the body (usually the very locus of creativity and communication) becomes inert and something of a prison. So it is that the sick person feels guilt. Whether at the naive level of wondering what-have-I-done-to-deserve-this? or in terms of a more sophisticated and existential perspective that will insist that nothing happens without some degree of intention on my part, that I am always an accomplice in my illness, guilty of my affliction, the separation from the world which sickness brings is real separation, real loss of community, and is, at the phenomenal level, a sort of excommunication.

Van den Berg, in *The Psychology of the Sickbed*, has described such an illness, an illness of no great seriousness or danger, which yet, in his description, brings out something of the similarity of the experience of illness and that of guilt. Having described the inital discovery of being sick upon awaking in the morning and determined to stay in bed, he says:

> Then, slowly, but irrevocably, a change, characteristic of the sickbed, established itself. I hear the day begin. From downstairs the sounds of household activities penetrate into the bedroom . . . What I am hearing is the beginning of my daily existence, with this difference, though, that now I have no function in it. In a way, I still belong completely to what happens downstairs; I take a share in the noises I hear, but at the same time everything passes me by, everything happens at a great distance. "Is Daddy ill?" a voice calls out; even at this early moment, it has ceased to consider that I can hear it. "Yes, Daddy is ill." A moment later the door opens and they come to say goodbye. They remain just as remote. The distance I measured in the sounds from downstairs appears even greater, if possible, now that they are at my bedside, with their fresh clean faces and lively gestures. Everything about them indicates the normal healthy day, the day of work and play, of street and school. The day outside the house, in which "outside" has acquired a new special meaning for me, a meaning emphasizing my exclusion . . .
>
> The world has shrunk to the size of my bedroom, or rather my bed. For even if I set foot on the floor it seems as if I am entering a *terra incognita*. Going to the bathroom is an unfriendly, slightly unreal, excursion. With the feeling of coming home I pull the blankets over me . . .
>
> The horizon in time too is narrowed. The plans of yesterday lose their meaning and their importance; they have hardly any real value. They seem more complicated, more exhausting, more foolish and ambitious than I saw them the day before. All that awaits me becomes tasteless, or even distasteful. The past seems saturated with trivialities. It appears to me that I hardly ever tackled my real tasks. Future and past lose their outlines; I withdraw from both and I live in the confined present of this bed which guards me against the things that were and those that will be . . . The present, while always serving the future, and therefore often being an effect of the past, becomes saturated with itself. As a patient I live with a useless body in a disconnected present."[8]

The Paschal Dynamic of Sickness

It is to such a sense of separation in the patient of disorder that the rite of anointing is addressed, just as the rite of penance is addressed to the like separation of the agent of disorder. And, as the object of the rite of penance is restoration to the body through a *metanoia* whose dynamic is baptismal and paschal, so the object of the rite of anointing can be understood as renewal of the baptismal anointing by which each of us is *christos* so that the suffering and separation of sickness become identified as participation in the *pascha Christi*. By such anointing, *anamnesis* is made of the passage of Christ through death to life and of the patient's consecration to this mystery. By such anointing, further, the suffering of the illness is oriented to a reopened future, a sense of movement in Christ through the present passion toward the kingdom. Sickness becomes a work, a work of learning in act that for those who are Christ's, there is no suffering that is not his. Thus the separation and humiliation of suffering become an invitation to a *conversio* from which one never returns to "former health"—one of the more regrettable phrases in the liturgies of anointing—but always moves into a deeper realization of life in the resurrection.

In the light of such an understanding of the anointing of affliction, it becomes considerably less important whether we see the sacrament as oriented toward healing or as oriented toward death. If we ask, "will the patient live?", the answer is a clear and triumphant "yes." This was established on the day of resurrection, and this is what it means to be an anointed one. But if we ask again, "will the patient die?", we must answer, still in accordance with the promise, "unless the *parousia* comes first, yes." The meaning of every illness is dying, and every healing is resurrection.

The sacrament is more than a struggle against illness. It is the sign of the conquest of death. It seeks not to palliate, to lull, to console, but to reveal, in the light of the Gospel, the meaning of sickness, and to consecrate it as a sign. For sickness itself is already a sign, rich with ambiguity, revealing both our problems and our resources. As Jacques Sarano says, "Sickness is the sign of that which we are, but it is this in two ways . . . The one *reduces* us to what we are (and nothing more); the other *calls* us to what we are (and nothing less)."[9]

As both retrospective and prospective, illness is always the passage-point, the threshold, between a dying and a living. Situating me between the life I have lived and the life I am for, sickness is *liminal* in an unusually personal and bodily way. And it is just that liminality that calls forth the sacrament of anointing for the illumination of its ambiguity and the articulation of the transition it marks and demands. This may be transition to accustomed life patterns assumed with a renewed and deepened understanding of myself and my vocation; it may be transition to a radically tranformed life; it may be transition to the glory of the kingdom. But a paschal valorization of the liminal condition need not and dare not limit the options. As symbolic structure, the liturgy of sickness has a broader scope than a mere ancillary therapeusis addressed to just this illness in just this patient. Sacramental and liturgical structures are more universal in their orientation. In the rites of affliction, indeed, we have neither a sacrament of the living nor a sacrament of the dead, but of the threshold between them. At this threshold, as in martyrdom, one finds oneself at the very heart of the mystery of one's being and of one's being in Christ. And there we can cry, in agony and exultation: "I am crucified with Christ, and behold, I live; and the life which I now live in the flesh, I live by the grace of the Son of God who loved me and gave himself for me."

Here, both for the patient and for the community wounded by this person's separation from it, the outrage of disorder is subsumed to the very ground of their life, the salvation of the cross. Here the loss of everything becomes a new mode of possessing salvation. To proclaim and to celebrate this is the purpose of the rites for the sick. Here as in all the tradition, the purpose of the rite is to reveal the presence of Christ.

The Interaction of Rite and Charism

But now we must return to a consideration of charismatic healing, for its end is the same. The difference between the sacrament of anointing and charismatic healing is not one of ultimate end. Both proclaim and reveal Christ and the power of his resurrection over all disorder. Both are instruments of God, and means of manifesting his glory. The covenant cultus, the sacramental economy, seeks to provide a Christian form of our living and dying. It must seek always to remain faithful both to the tradition and the tradition's dynamic of development. But it always aims at providing a continuity that can give the form of Christ to the wounds we sustain. Such a liturgical continuity manifests God, but does not contain him. Indeed, God is faithful to reveal his power in ways that are independent of this continuity, and which yet validate it by manifesting the power of him whom the tradition serves. On the other hand, it is life within the continuity, within the symbol complex, that enables us to recognize the source of the power of the charismatic, and thus the charismatic event.

What remains important is that sacramental continuity and charismatic discontinuity should vitalize each other in interaction, as the priests and the prophets of the Old Covenant, for without this the liturgy reverts to the law. Of the charism of healing there is, in fact, little to be said systematically, for it is not a systematic phenomenon. Our concern has been rather to show that it is God's sovereign power that is revealed in such phenomena, and not the unvarying content of his will for humanity. For most of us most of the time, it is the will of God that we should so live with ambiguity as to allow ourselves to trust in him and keep all options open to the power of his love. Illness, and not only serious illness, brings this ambiguity to a sharper focus than our living normally allows. To such ambiguity we can bring no more powerful sign than the renewal of the sign of our baptismal death and resurrection in the Anointed One. In this sign and in this assurance we can know that the life God gives is the life to which he calls us, and that the death which is the way to it—whether the death of missing two days' wages with a stinking cold or the death that will be the last death—is no longer ours but Christ's, and is the promise of his life.

Notes

1. Rites for the Sick (Washington, D.C.: International Committee on English in the Liturgy, 1971) 2. The original form of this chapter was

written before the appearance of the final form of the rite. The final text is much closer to the Tridentine definition than was this initial draft.

2. Cited by P. Palmer, *Sacraments and Forgiveness*, Sources of Christian Theology, vol. 2 (Westminster, MD: Newman Press, 1960) 310.

3. Ibid. 311-312.

4. Ibid. 307-308.

5. G. Dix, ed., *The Treatise on The Apostolic Tradition of St. Hippolytus of Rome* (London: S.P.C.K., 1968) 10, 12.

6. Palmer, *Sacraments* 278.

7. Although a reference to presbyteral anointing of the sick is found in the fifth century in Innocent I, Epistle 25 (Palmer, *Sacraments* 283), it is clear from the same document that lay anointing continued as well. It seems the more common opinion that the use of the term *sacramentum* in this text refers not to the presbyteral anointing, but to the oil itself. For the liturgical institutionalization of the James text, one must wait for the Carolingian period.

8. J.H. van den Berg, *The Psychology of the Sickbed* (Pittsburgh: Duquesne University Press, 1966) 24-25.

9. Jacques Sarano, *The Meaning of the Body* (Philadelphia: Westminster Press, 1966) 158.

5

The Liturgy of Reconciliation

"REPENT, AND BE BAPTIZED EVERY ONE OF YOU IN THE NAME OF JESUS Christ for the forgiveness of your sins; and you shall receive the gift of the Holy Spirit." So preached Peter at Pentecost, according to Acts 2, and for the first generation of Christians it was indeed baptism that accomplished the forgiveness of sins and the end of sin, once and for all. Still today in the creed we confess, "one baptism for the remission of sins." Nonetheless, already in the Pauline corpus and in Acts we can see the emerging recognition of the anomaly of postbaptismal disorder and the address of ecclesiastical discipline to it. Whatever the fundamental importance attached to baptism, the church was growing toward recognition of the need for ministering to Christians who fell into sin after baptism, and with this recognition came the beginnings of ritual reconciliation of the penitent.

Ritual reconciliation has two moments, the first focused on the separation occasioned by sin, the second focused on the reconciliation of the converted sinner to the community of faith. Like baptism, to the dignity of which reconciliation restores the penitent, the liturgy of reconciliation is a rite of *metanoia*, of conversion, moving from death to life, from sorrow to joy, from alienation to communion.

One Baptism and One Penance

This similarity of dynamic between baptism and penance was recognized already in *The Shepherd* of Hermas, an apocalyptic work written at Rome toward the middle of the second century. While there are more uncertainties surrounding this work than can be treated here, authorities seem to agree that it was Hermas who first gave expression to what was for following centuries a decisive characteristic of the discipline of penance at Rome, namely, that whereas forgiveness of sins committed after baptism was possible, such forgiveness could not be given repeatedly, but only once.[1] Like baptism itself, penance was *ephapax*, "once for all."

The principle of but one penance, later accepted also in Alexandria, Africa, Gaul, and Spain, eventually limited the old canonical penance to one of the so-called "last rites" performed on the death bed.[2] This development testifies not only to the severity of penitential life expected even after reconciliation, but also to the fear Christians had of falling back into sin after that one penance. The "once for all" character of solemn penance, once having found a place in ministry to the dying, was extended as well to the anointing of the sick, leaving the tradition that the anointing, too, could be given only once unless the patient, contrary to expectation, recovered.[3] Indeed, the liturgy of the anointing was itself accommodated to the penitential concern, and the texts accompanying the anointings spoke less of healing sickness than of forgiving sins.

Such a penitential understanding of the anointing of the sick, however, was no mere late medieval decadence. The fifth chapter of the Epistle of James, we know, has long served as a scriptural warrant for this anointing. Yet there, already, the expected fruit of that anointing, with the prayers of the presbyters, includes the forgiveness of any sins the sufferer may have committed. As noted in the previous chapter, the earliest commentary on that passage remaining to us, in Origen's second homily on Leviticus (PG 12.417), cites the James text within a discussion of penance. There is an important point here, I believe. The connection between penance and the anointing of the sick reveals the church's fundamentally therapeutic rather than juridical approach to sin.

Nor is the performance of canonical penance at the point of death quite the cheap solution that it might seem. Already in Hermas, it appears, the context of the limitation of penance to but one reconciliation is expectation of the imminent eschaton. If the world did not end as Hermas expected, there remained a sense of eschatological urgency associated with the sacrament of penance, a preparation for the coming of the end, which gained for penance a peculiar place in grave illness.

Nonetheless, admission to public penance at the approach of death was surely a secondary development from the earlier penitential practice, which played an important role in the shaping of the liturgical year. The relation of penance to baptism led to the framing of penitential exercises within the period preceding Easter. While the original stratum of the period we know as Lent seems to have been a time for the final honing of candidates for baptism, as early as the second decade of the fifth century we have the testimony of Epistle 25 of Innocent I (PL 20:551ff.) to assure us that at that time in Rome public penitents were reconciled on Thursday in Holy Week. At Milan, at the same period, reconciliation occurred on the following day, that which we know as Good Friday. In either case, it is clear that the concern was to accomplish the reconciliation so that the restored Christians could observe the full pascha and, together with the neophytes, receive the eucharist at that central festival.

Reconciliation on Maundy Thursday presumed the enrollment of penitents at the beginning of Lent. In the fifth century this was done on the Monday following the first Sunday of Lent,[4] but we now know the first day of Lent as Ash Wednesday, the Wednesday of the week preceding the first Sunday. Since the liturgy of this Wednesday establishes the penitential character of Lent, it may be appropriate to make a short detour to understand how the rite took its present shape.

Evolution of the Ash Wednesday Rite

One feature of this rich liturgy is its provision, following the sermon, for the imposition of ashes, the symbolic ceremony which gave this day its common name. The ceremony was preserved in the Roman Missal prior to the Second Vatican Council, but it preceded the eucharist and its scripture readings.[5] Following Vatican II, the revision of the Roman liturgy put the ceremony in this new position, allowing the homilist to comment on it, and it is this new arrangement which has been adopted in the *Book of Common Prayer* of the Episcopal Church.

Not infrequently, however, worshipers have questioned the appropriateness of the marking of the foreheads of the people with ashes so shortly after the explicit directive of Christ in the Gospel, "And when you fast, do not look dismal, like the hypocrites, for they disfigure their faces that their fasting may be seen by men . . . But when you fast, anoint your head and wash your face, that your fasting may not be seen by men but by your Father who is in secret . . ." It is ironic that liturgical revisions of the twentieth century, revisions made with the best of pastoral motives, should have posed this problem of conflict between the Gospel and the ceremony that gave this day its familiar name. More is involved, however, than just the inversion of the order of the distribution of ashes and the gospel reading.

The gospel assigned to Ash Wednesday, from the sixth chapter of Matthew, has been associated with this Wednesday since at least the fifth century. In that century the Bishop of Turin, Maximus, although opposed to some attempts to extend the fast to a total of seven weeks, notes that some of the faithful in his church begin their fast on the Wednesday before Lent because the gospel on this day contains the directions of the Lord regarding fasting.[6] At that time, although some churches were adding a week of *Quinquagesima*, this Wednesday was not yet the first day of Lent; the season of fasting still began on the following Sunday.

It was on the Sunday called *Quadragesima* ("Fortieth") that the forty-day period of fasting began—one still counted all the days, not just the fast days—and it was on the Monday after *Quadragesima* that those guilty of grave sins were admitted to the order of penitents, those who would spend the forty days in penitential exercises and would be solemnly restored to communion on Thursday in Holy Week. About a century or so later, so as to provide forty days of actual fasting, the enrollment of penitents was moved back to the previous Wednesday, and we may take it that Rome had already assigned to this day the same gospel as did Turin and our present rites. However, Rome did not sprinkle ashes on the penitents at their enrollment, neither on this day nor on the following Monday, the day when it seems the penitents were enrolled in the fifth century. There were no ashes where this gospel was read.

Although the association of ashes with enrollment as penitents was not uncommon outside Rome, our earliest clear evidence of the sprinkling of ashes on the penitents at their enrollment on Ash Wednesday is found in Germany in the tenth century.[7] This powerful ceremony of public (albeit temporary) exclusion from the Christian community came to an end when the penitents were shown out of the church while the choir sang an anthem based on the Genesis account of the ejection of Adam from Eden. The gospel passage read at the eucharist was the parable of the Pharisee and the Publican (Luke 18:9-14).[8]

While the formal exclusion of sinners may have continued longer in Germany than it did elsewhere, the rigor of such public penance was too heavy, and the formal enrollment of public penitents fell into desuetude, giving way to private penance. The ceremony of the sprinkling of ashes as a sign of penitence, however, continued on the Wednesday that opened the fast. It is in England, at the opening of the eleventh century, that Aelfric, Abbot of Eynsham, gives the earliest testimony to the sprinkling of ashes on all the faithful, not just public penitents. At the end of that century, at a council at Benevento, Pope Urban II made such a practice universal.[9] It is in the eleventh century, then, so far as we can tell, that the sprinkling of ashes came to precede a eucharist at which Matthew 6 was read, this having been the gospel for the day six centuries earlier when it was still four or five days before Lent.

The ceremony, however, seems to have involved a sprinkling of ashes on the heads of the faithful, not the marking of a cross with ashes on the forehead. Although clerics who wore the crowns of their heads shaved were marked with a cross on the tonsure, all the prayers and rubrics continued to speak of sprinkling the ashes on the head, and this ceremony, however suggestive of the repentance of the Ninevites (Jonah 3:6), would have involved no disfiguring of the faces of the faithful. While at some point this marking with the cross was extended to the foreheads of the laity, the ceremony continued to precede the gospel in which Christ urged against such display. It is only in our own day that the ceremony has come to follow after the gospel reading, presenting an appearance of conflict, a conflict unknown by tradition.

Separation and Reconciliation in Public Penance

The old rites for the exclusion of public penitents at the beginning of Lent and their reconciliation in Holy Week represent the solemnities from which subsequent forms of sacramental reconciliation have developed, and they deserve detailed description. In the medieval form of the rite, those to be admitted to penance knelt outside the church doors, clothed in the ragged or harsh clothing that would characterize their sorrow, their heads bowed to the ground. After the bishop had blessed the ashes, a procession led to the center of the nave where a seat was prepared for the bishop. The presbyters divided into two choirs, standing before and on either side of the bishop, while archpresbyters called the penitents from their several jurisdictions to enter. They filed into the church, each holding a lighted candle like that given at baptism, and prostrated before the bishop, between the two choirs of the clergy. An archpresbyter sprinkled them with water, and the bishop put ashes on the head of each, saying, "remember that you are dust, and to dust you shall return; do penance and you shall have eternal life," while, one by one, their candles were extinguished. Then, while the penitents and clergy prostrated, seven penitential psalms and a litany were sung, after which the clergy arose and the bishop prayed over the penitents. After a sermon to the penitents on Adam's exclusion from paradise, the bishop took one of the penitents by the hand and, all the other penitents following, ejected them from the church as was Adam from Paradise, while the choir sang, "In the sweat of your brow shall you eat bread, said the Lord to Adam, till you return to the earth, for out of it you were taken; dust you are, and to dust you shall return." Over the penitents, kneeling in the porch, the bishop spoke a final admonition, urging them to give themselves to prayer and fasting, pilgrimage and almsgiving, until their return on Thursday of Holy Week. Then the doors of the church were shut before their faces, and the bishop, clergy, and others proceeded to the Mass.

Having made confession to the priests and given account of their lenten exile, it was again before the doors of the church that the penitents assembled on Maundy Thursday, in their ragged garb and barefoot, holding their unlighted candles. In the choir the bishop and clergy prostrated and recited again the seven penitential psalms and litany. The litany was interrupted at three points. At the first two interruptions two subdeacons with lighted candles went to the doors and spoke words of hope to the waiting penitents, then extinguished their candles before the penitents and returned to the sanctuary. At the third interruption, at the *Agnus Dei*, it was a senior deacon with a large lighted candle who was sent to the penitents waiting outside the door with their unlighted candles. Having sung, "Lift up your heads, for your redemption draws near," he lighted the candles of all the penitents, candles that had been extinguished at the beginning of Lent. The deacon returned to the choir while the litany resumed with the *Agnus Dei*, and the bishop then arose from his prostration and, with the other ministers, went to the center of the nave where, as on Ash Wednesday, a faldstool had been prepared for him. The archdeacon addressed to him a long announcement of the time of reconciliation which again draws out the connection between penance and baptism:

> For although because of the riches of God's goodness and piety no time is without it, yet now the remission of sins is more bountiful through forgiveness, and the admission of the reborn is more abundant through grace. We receive increase by those being reborn, we grow by those who have returned. Waters cleanse, tears cleanse. From the first comes joy for the admission of those who have been called, from the latter happiness for the absolution of the penitents.

At the conclusion of the address, the bishop went with his attendants to the door where the penitents waited, and called them three times, "Come, come, come, my sons; hear me, I will teach you the fear of the Lord." As he returned to the church the choir began to sing Psalm 34 with the antiphon, "Look to him and be radiant, so your faces shall never be ashamed," and all the penitents followed the bishop to the center of the nave where they prostrated before him. When the archdeacon had vouched for the sincerity of their repentance, the bishop began the long series of prayers for their release that concludes in the formal absolution, a text which finds echos in one of the forms for absolution in the American *Book of Common Prayer*.

> The Lord Jesus Christ, who saw fit to purge the sins of the whole world by handing himself over and by pouring out his immaculate Blood, and who said to His disciples: Whatsoever you will bind on earth will be bound in heaven, and whatsoever you will loose on earth will be loosed in heaven: among whose number he wanted me, though unworthy, to be a minister . . . may He absolve you through my ministry from all your sins, whatever either by thought, or speech, or by deed you have done negligently, through the intervention of His holy Blood, which is poured out for the remission of sins.

When the penitents had been sprinkled with water and censed, the bishop said, "Rise up you who sleep, rise from the dead, and Christ will give you light." With that, their reconciliation was completed with a final blessing.

This long description has been condensed from the thirteenth-century pontifical of William Durandus,[10] but, although his text reflects some development over earlier forms, it is certain that by his time this impressive rite had ceased to be performed with any regularity. Indeed, on Ash Wednesday, after the description of the solemn expulsion of the public penitents, we find the actual administration of ashes to the clergy and people before the beginning of Mass.

Transition to Private Penance

By the time of Durandus the old rites of public penance had long been displaced by private penance, which began to enter the life of the church on the continent late in the sixth century. This form, deriving from the spiritual direction customary in monasteries, knew no limitation to but one reconciliation as was the case with canonical penance. The tradition of private penance is known to us through manuals called *penitentials*. Carried to the continent in 590 by Columban and his party of twelve missionary monks, the Irish penitential tradition took root there and flourished with the establishment of further Celtic monasteries. While the early penitentials, continental or Irish, are but pastoral manuals detailing the tariff penances appropriate to various sins and the status of the sinner (e.g., whether clerical or lay), two centuries later their Frankish descendants include directions for the actual carrying out of the rite. After an initial instruction from the confessor on the importance of confession and examination of the penitent's faith in the resurrection, the penitent confesses his or her sins. Then both penitent and confessor lie prostrate before the altar and recite verses from the penitential psalms. Next, having further questioned the penitent regarding faith and willingness to do penance, the appropriate fasts or other devotions are assigned for a given period. Just prior to the assignment of penance, however, a rather surprising directive is found in one important source, a penitential from Fleury from the last quarter of the eighth century:

> Then, if he has criminal matters,[11] either a presbyter or a deacon shall say the collects over his head, and afterward, prostrate on the ground, he shall be commended to the Lord God of heaven, and they shall say the passage, "Confirm this, O God" (Ps 68:28b).

Here it seems that the reconciliation is due more to the confession itself than to any specific act of reconciliation on the part of the church. Indeed, after reciting the pentitential psalm verses, the confessor is directed to ask, "whether he believes that through his confession itself he obtains pardon." This passage suggests that absolution was given only if grave sins (*causas criminales*) were confessed, and, further, that the absolution was precatory rather than declarative, being in the form of a series of collects such as those recited by the bishop in canonical penance. It is also interesting that these could be recited by a deacon, at least if no priest were available, a provision made also in a penitential of St. Gall.[12] After the assignment of penance, the penitent is dismissed with the verse, "The Lord keep thee from all evil" (Ps 121:7).

It is from about the same period that we begin to encounter analogous rites in the Byzantine tradition, included within similar penitential manuals. The earliest such rite is in the *Canonarium* of a deacon and monk called "John, the son of Obedience." There the penance rite opens with Psalm 70 and Trisagion and prayer, recited together by the confessor and penitent. The confession followed, with further interrogation by the confessor. There is a precatory absolution, namely, a prayer for absolution, recited over the prostrate penitent, and, finally, the fixing of the penance.[13] The similarity of these oriental forms to those of the same period in Gaul raises the question of the relationship between the two. There is no question of verbal connections between the Frankish and Byzantine penitential forms, but they do seem to come out of a similar background and reflect similar structures. In both cases we are in the presence of an ascetical discipline, practiced with some regularity as a means of spiritual development. Such an understanding of penance as no longer the single rescue allowed for sin after baptism, but rather a salutary, indeed necessary, spiritual discipline achieved institutionalization at the Fourth Lateran Council in 1215. While we should not minimize the profound change effected by that council, it, too, was a moment in a process. During the eleventh and twelfth centuries increasing attention was paid to the authority of presbyters to absolve, a function of the growing identification of *sacerdotium* with the presbyterate rather than the episcopate, and declarative forms of absolution became more common. At the

Lateran Council it was established that every Christian must confess and receive communion at least annually, and the council even ordered confession prior to the first communion of children who had come to the age of responsibility. Such a regulation makes it clear that we are confronted no longer with the reconciliation of those who had been excluded, even temporarily, from the communion of the church, but are rather speaking of penance as a normal dimension of Christian piety.

The Ritual Space

The shift away from the original meaning of the rite vastly increased the numbers of confessions to be heard, and this in turn had a telling impact on the liturgical form taken by the rite. Now there was little liturgical context such as had been supplied by the recitation of the penitential psalms in common by penitent and confessor, and in following centuries significant interaction between penitent and confessor was increasingly eroded.

When the rite called for those psalms to be recited by penitent and priest lying prostrate before the altar, the normal place for the rite was at the entrance to the sanctuary. The formula of absolution, when it became declarative, was administered with the imposition of the hands of the priest. The early oriental rites sometimes call for the priest to kiss the penitent.[14] The whole atmosphere of close interpersonal relationship may sometimes have been seen as problematic when the penitent was a woman, but the dangers of celibate priests confronting emotionally vulnerable (and perhaps morally compromised) women achieved panic proportions in northern Italy in the sixteenth century. Charles Borromeo, Archbishop of Milan from 1560 to 1584, is usually credited with the invention of the confessional closet, a contrivance which effectively protects penitents from intimate contact with their confessors, separating them by a wall in which is placed a small window, covered by a metal grill. This, of course, put an end to the imposition of the confessor's hand, but the priest was still directed to hold his right hand extended toward the now untouchable penitent throughout the formula of absolution.

In consequence of the reforms since Vatican II, the ubiquitous closets have for the most part fallen into desuetude, replaced by more commodious rooms that allow for face to face encounter. While these reconciliation rooms afford opportunity to address every aspect of the rite of reconciliation, in some cases (one thinks especially of the glass edicules found in the naves of some churches in Paris) they breathe an atmosphere less suggestive of a liturgical space than of the psychotherapist's office. Sacramental reconciliation will be tragically impoverished if it ceases to draw on the power of ritual action.

Penance in the Reformation

The Reformation itself made little immediate change in the understanding of penance in England. The people were no longer required to make confession before receiving communion, but prior to the Reformation they had for the most part done either only once a year. The immediate agenda of the reforms in this matter focused on making communion once again central to the eucharist. Therefore, every attempt was made to encourage the regular communion of the people. One aspect of this was the inclusion of a general confession and absolution in the vernacular communion rite inserted into the Latin Mass in 1548 and subsequently included in the *Book of Common Prayer*.[15] Such a confession and absolution were new to the text of the liturgy itself, although in later medieval use such devotions were found in monastic customaries and, in the vernacular, in some parishes.[16]From 1614 these were ordered prior to the communion of the people by the *Rituale Romanum*, a formal inclusion of them in the Latin rite that superceded the vernacular usage. The responsibility of pastors for the discipline of the church and the authority of priests to absolve were never doubted by the English reformers. Indeed, the *Book of Common Prayer* as early as 1549 announced the hope and intention of restoring public penance. While they never displaced the *Commination against Sinners* on Ash Wednes day, some forms of public penance were in fact devised in the sixteenth century, though they seem to have placed little emphasis on solemn reconciliation. That emphasis was to be found in the rite for the reconciliation of apostates issued in the seventeenth century by Archbishop Laud.[17] This rite, extended over three Sundays, demonstrated both the relation of reconciliation to baptism and eucharist and the therapeutic concern common to penance and ministrations to the sick.

Those traditional concerns are evident as well in the recent reforms of the rites of penance. The Roman *Ordo Paenitentiae* issued late in 1973 provides for the reconciliation of penitents in three forms: (a) the reconciliation of an individual penitent, (b) the reconciliation of several penitents with individual confessions and absolutions, and (c) the reconciliation of many penitents with a general confession and absolution. In the latter case, individual confession is expected to follow later, underscoring the healing function of confession even when one's relation to the community has been restored. In all the forms, the priest is presented as healer, not as judge, and care is taken to set confession and absolution in the context of the proclamation of the word of God, by contrast to the rather stark efficiency of the form used prior to Vatican II.

It was this form—an opening blessing, the confession, counsel and assignment of penance, absolution and final blessing and dismissal—which had been adopted in Anglican use as well since the later nineteenth century. The form first appeared in a more or less official publication of the Episcopal Church in a small liturgical and devotional manual for members of the Armed Forces during World War II, but it had long since been published in privately issued devotional manuals and has been the form known to virtually all in the church who made any regular use of sacramental reconciliation. It is substantially reproduced as the first of two forms in the present American *Book of Common Prayer*, retained because of its familiarity and brevity. A second form in the Prayer Book, recognizing that a larger liturgical context was desirable, was informed by current Byzantine use and the new Roman rite for an individual confession. It seeks to keep before the penitent the dual meaning of *confessio* or *exomologesis* as at once a confession of our own sin and of our faith in God and in the redemption accomplished for us on the cross.

The role of faith in reconciliation, like the role of faith in baptism, seems central in the early rites. Our penitential exercises are not, as much past theological discussion suggested, works offered to God in satisfaction for our sins. Rather, like catechesis, they represent the developmental working out of our conversion, our response to the divine initiative revealed in Christ. The revelation of God in Jesus Christ and his accomplishment of our redemption in the paschal mystery are at once the condemnation of sin and its conquest. To perceive this is to lay hold on eternal life, but to learn to live with and by this perception is the occupation of a lifetime. The reality of our redemption and our failure to live redemption fully are the terms of the divine dialogue through which we seek to become who we are. In the better parts of its long tradition, the liturgy of reconciliation is the sign of this dialogue, for it is the continual expression of the passage of our so mishandled history into the redemptive mystery of the cross, there to become in us the gift of his risen life.

Notes

1. Hermas, *The Shepherd*, Mandate IV.iii.6.

2. For an example from Spain in the sixth century, cf. M. Férotin, ed., *Le Liber Ordinum*, Monumenta Ecclesiae Liturgica, vol. 5 (Paris: Librarie de Firmin-Didot et Cie, 1904) cols. 87-92, and n. 2 on col. 86. At this early date, however, it is unlikely that admission to penance was limited to those near death.

3. Ivo of Chartres in the twelfth century (along with many others) considered the anointing to be, in fact, the rite of public penance. Bernhard Poschmann, *Penance and the Anointing of the Sick*, Francis Courtney, trans. (New York: Herder and Herder, 1964) p. 256, quotes Ivo: "the anointing of the sick is the sacrament of public penance, and Augustine and Ambrose testify that like baptism it cannot be repeated."

4. So J. Jungmann, *The Early Liturgy to the Time of Gregory the Great* (Notre Dame: University of Notre Dame Press, 1959) 245-246.

5. An arrangement retained still in the *Lutheran Book of Worship*.

6. DACL 22:2136.

7. Reginon of Prüm, *De eccl. disciplinis* I.291 (PL 132:245).

8. PRG XCIX.67. [Cyrille Vogel, Reinhard Elze, eds., *Le Pontifical Romano-Germanique du dixième siècle*, vol. 2, Studi e testi vol. 227 (Città del Vaticano: Biblioteca Apostolica Vaticana, 1963) 20.]

9. H. Thurston, s.v. "Ash Wednesday," *The Catholic Encyclopedia*, vol. 1 (New York, 1913) 775.

10. Michel Andrieu, *Le Pontifical de Guillaume Durand*, vol. 3 of *Le Pontifical romain au moyen-âge*, Studi e testi, vol. 88 (Città del Vaticano: Biblioteca Apostolica Vaticana, 1940) 552-569.

11. *Postea si causas criminales habet.* John T. McNeill and Helena M. Gamber, *Medieval Handbooks of Penance: A Translation of the Principal Libri Poenitentiales and Selections from Related Documents*(New York: Columbia University Press, 1938) 282, render the phrase: "If later he offends criminally." The translation here is that given in Appendix B of Polycarp Sherwood, O.S.B., ed., *Penance: The Ministry of Reconciliation. Resonance*, no. 2 (St. Meinrad, IN: St. Meinrad School of Theology, 1966) 128.

12. McNeill and Gamber, *Medieval Handbooks* 284.

13. Louis Ligier, S.J., *Introduzione alla liturgia orientale della penitenza. Ad usum privatum auditorum* (Rome: Pontificium Institutum Orientalium Studiorum, 1968) 114-117.

14. PG 88:1892 A, 1921 C.

15. R.C.D. Jasper and G.J. Cuming, *Prayers of the Eucharist: Early and Reformed*, 3rd rev. ed. (New York: Pueblo Publishing Co., 1987) 226-231.

16. See Josef Jungmann, *The Mass of the Roman Rite*, trans., Francis A. Brunner, vol. 2 (New York: Benziger Brothers, Inc., 1955) 371.

17. Vernon Staley, *Hierurgia Anglicana*, Part 3 (London: De la More Press, 1904) 10-15.

6

History and Eschatology in the Primitive Pascha

IT HAS BECOME SOMETHING OF A COMMONPLACE AMONG LITURGISTS that the primitive eschatological time-sense of liturgical observance, a proleptic experience of the resurrection associated liturgically with the primitive pascha and the observance of Sunday throughout the year, underwent a rather abrupt historicization in the fourth century. This change, which Gregory Dix associated especially with the liturgy of Jerusalem as it developed in the time of Cyril, introduced a commemorative dimension virtually unknown to the ante-Nicene church (according to this view).[1]This accommodation to a historical time model is often represented as an aspect of the accommodation of the church to its new public life in consequence of Constantine's edicts, and this in turn can be made to seem some sort of failure of nerve on the part of the church, an acceptance of historical time as fundamental so as to make the crucifixion and resurrection seem mere past events, however significant.

This interpretation, it seems to me, is in need of considerable qualification in both its assertions. It does not appear that historical commemoration in the liturgy is a function of new outlooks in the fourth century, nor does it appear that that period saw a radical decay of eschatology in spirituality. Such a need for qualification, at any rate, is my concern in this consideration of liturgical time in the earlier centuries of the church's life, and especially as regards the primitive pascha.

Cyrille Vogel of the University of Strasbourg once observed that what is astonishing about the Christian year is not that it developed so slowly, but that it developed at all, since every celebration of the eucharist is celebration of the life, death, and resurrection of the Lord.[2] This is true enough, but the earliest accounts of the eucharist, the breaking of bread on the first day of the week, the emergence of the designation of that day as the Eighth Day, or even earlier as the Day of the Lord, does indeed suggest that Sunday assemblies were dominated by a powerful sense of being in and with the risen Lord and standing in expectation of the parousia—namely, that the weekly gathering of the church was in an eschatological rather than a historical and commemorative time model. Certainly, even through the fourth century, the early church shows little concern for point-for-point recapitulation of the history of the saving work of Christ. This is perhaps most clear in the matter of ascension and Pentecost, "events" for which Acts 1 provides a sufficient historical timetable, but which resisted liturgical commemoration as historical events in some places right to the last decade of the fourth century or even later. In the first century, we see overt evidence of no annual celebrations at all.

The primitive church quite clearly took the week, not the year, as the significant liturgical cycle. Sunday was the primary celebration of the resurrection, the day on which—week by week—the church gathered in the Spirit to be with him who makes himself known in the breaking of bread, and to enjoy the foretaste of his kingdom. It would be senseless to describe this Eighth Day kept every week as a "little Easter," for it was (and for much of the church continued to be, right on up to the third century) the fundamental celebration and liturgical experience of the resurrection.

The Passover of Christ

But if every Sunday was not a little Easter, what is one to say of Easter itself? In the first instance, it must be said that the question is ill-posed, for the word *Easter* belongs to a much later stage of the evolution of the festival and carries with it presuppositions that are inappropriate to the primitive observance. We should rather ask when and how did the Christian observance of pascha appear alongside the weekly celebration of the resurrection, and what was the content of the annual celebration that distinguished it from that weekly observance? Given the sparseness of our information as regards the time of origin of the Christian observance of pascha, we will do best, perhaps, to begin with the latter question, that of the content of the celebration. Here it is fairly clear that the overwhelmingly predominant theme of pascha in the ante-Nicene period is the passion of Christ; the earliest pascha was, in fact, just such a historical commemoration of the passion of Christ (as distinguished from the resurrection) as is commonly asserted to have emerged only in the later fourth century. This can easily, however, be read as an overstatement, and needs qualification. Just as the Sunday celebration of each week included the passion as one dimension of its celebration of the resurrection, so the annual celebration of the pascha did not exclude the resurrection from its theology; but what distinguished the paschal observance from that of the ordinary Sunday was that the pascha was a historical commemoration determined by the anniversary of the crucifixion. A work of the second century from Asia Minor, *Epistula Apostolorum*, has the risen Lord command the apostles, "and *you* therefore celebrate the remembrance of my death, i.e., the passover."[3]

Indeed, it was common up to the time of Augustine to argue the etymological derivation of *pascha* from the Greek *paschein*, "to suffer."[4] So Melito of Sardis in the second half of the second century could write: "What is the pasch? Its name is derived from what happened, from the verb 'to suffer,' to be suffering."[5] The same etymology is found in Lactantius, in a paschal homily derived from Hippolytus, and in a tractate of the pseudo-Origen (now assigned to Gregory of Elvira).[6] Even apart from this popular etymology, other writers assign the commemoration of the passion as the content of the paschal celebration. Tertullian in a well-known passage from *De baptismo* says: "The pascha affords a more solemn day for baptism, when also the passion of the Lord, in which we are baptized, was completed."[7] Again, the pseudo-Cyprianic author of *De pascha computus* writes: "We celebrate the pascha in commemoration of the passion of the Son of God."[8] It is the same in one of Origen's homilies on Isaiah: "There is now a multitude of people on account of the Preparation day, and especially on the Sunday which commemorates Christ's passion. For the resurrection of the Lord is not celebrated once in the year, but also always every eighth day."[9] It is, then, this commemoration of the passion of the Lord that in the first instance distinguishes the pascha from the regular Sunday celebration of the resurrection.

A second distinguishing characteristic of the pascha is that it is closely tied to a fast. Contrary to the usual practice of weekly fasts on Wednesday and Friday only, the pascha on Sunday is preceded by a fast on the previous day, the Sabbath on which fasting was customarily forbidden. Indeed, so integral is the relation of the fast to the paschal celebration that the celebration will be referred to again and again in terms of the "ending of the fast." This fast, we learn from Irenaeus, was variously observed—by some for one day (which would seem to have been the Saturday), by others for two days, by some for more than two days, and by yet others for forty hours spanning roughly the whole time that the Lord lay in the tomb.[10]

The third distinction of the pascha from ordinary Sundays is that the pascha is a pernocturnal observance. While it was once common teaching among liturgists that the primitive church regularly celebrated the weekly eucharist in the early hours of Sunday morning after spending the night in vigil, more recent opinion has recognized the unlikelihood of such a rigorous regimen.[11] On the contrary, there is every reason to believe that for the better part of the ante-Nicene church this extended nocturnal observance was a peculiarity of the paschal liturgy. It is widely accepted that at Rome in the time of Hippolytus, that is, in the early third century, this was a vigil lasting through the night until cockcrow. At that time the celebration of baptism began, and, when all the neophytes had been received by the bishop with the imposition of hands and a final anointing, the observance was completed with the celebration of the eucharist and the first communion of the newly baptized. While it is by no means unlikely that this would have brought the service near the time of sunrise, there is in the evidence no suggestion that this particular result was intended or sought. Indeed, one might ask whether the beginning of this nocturnal celebration had as its object a keeping of vigil throughout the hours of darkness. Was it this watching for the resurrection that was of primary concern, or can we see behind the developed paschal vigil the nocturnal celebration of the passover as it had been kept by the Jews in the light of the full moon since the days of their nomadism? Such seems clearly to be the case in our earliest description of the paschal vigil, that found in the second century *Epistula Apostolorum.*[12]

Historical Priority of Quartodecimanism

This question brings us up against one of the more difficult problems in the whole history of the pascha, namely, the relation of the Catholic pascha to the practice of the Quartodecimans of Asia. The issue comes to light for the first time in the episcopate of Victor at Rome in the last decade of the second century, though the controversy may be closely related to another reported by Eusebius soon after the middle of the century, but of which he tells us practically nothing beyond establishing the fact that the pascha was being celebrated at that time in Laodicea. In any case, the problem in the time of Victor concerned the allegedly deviant practice of the churches of Asia in keeping the pascha on the fourteenth day of the lunar month without regard to the day of the week on which it might fall.

Just how this variation of practice became a matter of controversy is not clear from Eusebius' treatment of it, but he does report that synods on the matter were held in Palestine, Rome, Pontus, Gaul, and Osrhoene. All these agreed that "the mystery of the Lord's resurrection from the dead should never be celebrated on any other day but Sunday, and that on this day only we should observe the end of the paschal fasts."[13]

It was at this point that the variant practice of Asia became a matter of overt dissent, and the resolve of those churches to maintain their local practice was communicated to Victor at Rome by Polycrates of Ephesus in a long epistle claiming a tradition for the Quartodeciman practice reaching back to John the Apostle.[14] In this connection, it is worth reminding ourselves, perhaps, that it is in the Johannine tradition that the passion of the Lord is situated on the Preparation of the Passover, the fourteenth of the lunar month, the Synoptics suggesting rather that the day was the First Day of Unleavened Bread, the fifteenth of the lunar month (though it was the Preparation of the Sabbath, i.e., Friday).

Victor, at least, was insufficiently impressed by the Ephesine claims for apostolic authority, an authority claimed by almost everyone for almost anything in the second century. Upon receipt of Polycrates' letter, Victor excommunicated the churches of Asia and urged other bishops to take the same action. Irenaeus, who had presided over the synod in Gaul, took exception to Victor's strong action and wrote to him, urging him to reverse it and recalling to him the more liberal of his predecessors in the Roman see. "Among these also," writes Irenaeus, "were the presbyters before Soter who presided over the Church which you now guide—I mean Anicetus and Pius, Hyginus and Telesphorus and Sixtus." Of these bishops of Rome whose pontificates reach back from the accession of Soter in 165 to around 116, Irenaeus continues:

> They neither observed it themselves, nor did they permit those after them to do so. And yet though not observing it, they were nonetheless at peace with those who came to them from the parishes in which it was observed; although this observance was more opposed to those who did not observe it. But none were ever cast out on account of this form; but the presbyters before thee who did not observe it, sent the eucharist to those other parishes who observed it. And when the blessed Polycarp was at Rome in the time of Anicetus, and they disagreed a little about certain other things, they immediately made peace with one another, not caring to quarrel over this matter. For neither could Anicetus persuade Polycarp not to observe what he had always observed with John the disciple of the Lord, and the other apostles with whom he had associated; neither could Polycarp persuade Anicetus to observe it, as he said that he ought to follow the customs of the presbyters that had preceded him. But though matters were in this shape, they communed together, and Anicetus conceded the administration of the eucharist in the church to Polycarp, manifestly as a mark of respect. And they parted from each other in peace, both those who observed, and those who did not, maintaining the peace of the whole church.[15]

John W. Tyrer, although he has shown a great sensitivity to the ambiguity of this document, nonetheless sees the difference between these early Romans and such Asians as Polycarp as only a difference in the time of the observance of the pascha.[16] I must confess, however, that I find his argument less than compelling. It seems to me that the clear implication of Irenaeus' letter is that, prior to Soter (i.e., before 165), the pasch was not observed at Rome at all, and that this was a more grievous conflict of traditions than the mere disagreement about the date that had so undone Victor. Even such an interpretation, of course, would speak only for Rome itself, and that excellent city has always been notoriously slow in accepting festivals from other quarters, and has not been noted for inventiveness in matters of heortology.[17]Yet even in the light of the possible peculiarity of Rome in the matter before us, it is difficult to avoid the conclusion that the Christian observance of the pascha had its beginnings in the Quartodeciman form, that it was a Christian continuation of the Old Testament celebration of Passover, an observance of the day of Preparation (the anniversary of the crucifixion) by fasting, and a nocturnal feast in which the eucharist replaced the passover meal. Such a eucharist, like every eucharist, would inescapably speak of and to the presence of the risen Lord in the midst of his people; it would celebrate the resurrection and proclaim the resurrection as it had ever since the road to Emmaus.

However, for just this reason it would constitute a severe problem for the primitive Christian understanding of time, for it would draw this celebration of the resurrection away from the Sunday of its observance, away from the eschatological day, the Day of the Lord, and would re-situate the resurrection in the framework of an anniversary, an annual commemoration of an event in the historical past. Such a change would do serious violence to the theology of the resurrection itself, for the resurrection of Christ is the principle of the New Age and cannot be reduced to a past event. While the passion of the Lord can be situated historically, the resurrection opens on the metahistorical presence of the Lord, and this is celebrated on the eschatological Eighth Day. An annual celebration, on the other hand, is virtually bound, by the very length of the annual cycle, to seem more commemorative; and when its primary focus is on the anniversary of the passion, this historical-commemorative character predominates. The conflict of history and eschatology should not be sought in the altered situation of the church and the empire in the fourth century, but in the very emergence of the annual celebration of the pascha as commemoration of the passion. It was this conflict between the week and the year as the basic frame of liturgical experience that required the accommodation of the latter cycle to the former so that the annual observance would conclude on Sunday.

Isidore of Seville, writing in the earlier decades of the seventh century, recognized the Quartodeciman origin of the pascha and attributed to the Council of Nicaea the establishment of the Catholic pascha on the Sunday falling between the fourteenth and twenty-first days of the moon.[18] Actually, of course, this Sunday pascha was widespread in the second century, even if we cannot see it as of equal antiquity with the Quartodeciman practice, as did Baumstark.[19] The Catholic solution was to keep the annual celebration, but to shift it so far as necessary in order to terminate the fast and celebrate the eucharist always on a Sunday. It is for this reason that the texts speak so consistently of the "ending of the paschal fasts," and manifest relatively little concern with when the fast is begun or how long it lasts. By the third century, the evidence for the fast is much clearer, the normal fast being the Friday and the Saturday before the paschal eucharist, though in certain circumstances it was understandable if one only fasted on Saturday. This was, as Tertullian notes, the only Sabbath of the year on which fasting was allowed (though he reveals with some alarm that the distinction is beginning to break down.)[20] The preference of Saturday over Friday as the one day on which to fast reflects the idea of the paschal eucharist terminating the fast as could be seen in the one-day observance of the Quartodecimans. A further consequence of the Catholic solution to the Pascha/Sunday problem would be the setting of the nocturnal vigil and eucharist of the Quartodeciman practice in the night from Saturday to Sunday. The whole point of the change was to situate the termination of the fast, that is, the eucharist, on a Sunday, but fasting on Sunday was unthinkable. Therefore, the fast must be through Saturday and its concluding nocturnal assembly must now pass through the night into the early hours of the morning.

As for the time when this Catholic solution was forged, we really have no definitive evidence, but Karl Holl, followed more recently by Marcel Richard, has presented a strong argument for seeing this development as a function of the establishment of the Gentile episcopate at Jerusalem around 135.[21] It has been argued above that it was not established at Rome before 165, but (for reasons adduced above) this need not mean that it had not occurred elsewhere at an earlier time. From whatever time, however, it would seem to be an adjustment of the historical-commemorative pascha of the Quartodeciman type to the original eschatological expectation of the Christian people, and at the same time a settling of eschatological expectation to a sense of linear history, of a Christian mission rooted in the *ephapax* of Calvary.

Pascha as Passage

This brings us to the remaining distinction between the pascha and ordinary Sundays in the second century, namely, establishing the annual celebration as an especially solemn time for baptism. Already in the middle of the century, Justin Martyr describes for us a baptismal eucharist and contrasts this to the regular Sunday observance.[22] Nothing in the passage, however, suggests a particular time of year for the baptismal eucharist. Since he would have written in the pontificate of either Pius or Anicetus, our previous argument would militate against assuming that Justin's baptismal eucharist is the pascha. Very early, however, and perhaps from the beginning of the paschal observance at Rome, the solemn administration of baptism becomes the great sacrament of the passion and resurrection of the Lord. As Christ had spoken of his passion as his baptism, and as Paul had spoken of our baptismal burial and rising with him, so it was inexorable that this rite should find the place in the paschal celebration that Tertullian assigns it at the end of the century, and that it should begin to add further theological dimension to our understanding of the paschal mystery.

Baptism is a sacrament of initiation and as such belongs to that somewhat broader category of ritual phenomena designated as "rites of passage." While one must be careful not to allow van Gennep's term or its broad acceptance by anthropologists and historians of religion to become a primary theological datum, his and other studies of such rites of transition help us to understand a growing shift of emphasis in the theology of the pascha related to the establishment of the feast as the primary occasion of baptism, a shift reflected in a change in comments on the etymology of the term.

We have referred above to the popularity in the ante-Nicene church of the false etymology that derived *pascha* from the Greek verb *paschein*, "to suffer." In the ante-Nicene period there were, however, such Alexandrians as Clement and Origen, who took from Philo of Alexandria an understanding of pascha as *diabasis*, *transitus*, "passage," a concept that Philo had treated as spiritual renewal, a passage from carnal passions to the exercise of virtue.[23] Here the emphasis in the pascha is not on the slaying of the lamb and the marking of the doors with its blood, but on the exodus from Egypt, the passage from slavery to freedom. Such a *transitus* interpretation of pascha is found again in northern Italy, in Gaudentius of Brescia, but especially in Ambrose.[24] The latter, building his themes from Philo's understanding of pascha as *diabasis-transitus*, relates baptism to the crossing of the Red Sea by way of Paul's baptismal typology in 1 Corinthians 10. By this development of baptismal typology in relation to the understanding of pascha, the theology of the paschal mystery reaches its fullness. The deliverance of the Hebrews by the blood of the lamb and their passage through the Red Sea to freedom, all this is fulfilled in Christ's own *transitus* from this world to the Father, a *metabasis* (as John 13:1 has it) in which we have been made to participate by being baptized into his pascha, passing with him and in him from death to life, from slavery to freedom, from sin to grace. Such is the full development, expressed also in Augustine, of the patristic theology of the paschal liturgy, a liturgy which, from its beginnings in the second century (or perhaps even the first) as a historical commemoration of the victorious passion and death of the Lord, has become the sacramental prolepsis of the eschaton, a process that is almost the exact opposite of that described by Dix: "that universal transposition of the liturgy from an eschatological to an historical interpretation of redemption, which is the outstanding mark left by the fourth century on the history of Christian worship."[25]

Neither an emphasis on historical commemoration as over against eschatological expectation of the parousia nor an observance focused on the passion and death of the Lord as distinguished from the Sunday celebration of the resurrection can be assigned to the radical transformation of the life of the church in the fourth century. The latter distinction is a function of the former, and that in turn is inherent in our Christian condition. Both the witness of Polycrates and what Irenaeus says of Polycarp give us reason to suspect that from the time of the Apostle John we have been living with this dialectic between eschatology and history. We always live between *marana tha*, that prayer for the coming of the Lord which is somehow already a shout of greeting, and *maran atha*, the confession that the Lord has come, a focus on the *ephapax* of God's ultimate act in history and its centrality. We always live, this is to say, between memory and hope, between his coming and his coming; and the present which is the threshold between these, between memory and hope, between past and future, this present is the locus of the presence of him who is at once Lord of history and its consummation. The remembrance of his passion and the recognition of his glory are integral to one another, and have been from the beginning. Simple liturgical expression of this rich interplay of history and eschatology, however, would seem to be something of a problem, and has been from the beginning.

Notes

1. Gregory Dix, *The Shape of the Liturgy* (London: Dacre, 1945) 347-360.

2. Cyrille Vogel, *Introduction aux sources de l'histoire du culte chrétien au moyen âge* (Spoletto: Centro italiano di studi sull'alto medioevo, 1966) 264, n. 77. This particular statement is no longer found in the excellent revision and translation of Vogel's work by Niels Rasmussen and William Storey, *Medieval Liturgy: An Introduction to the Sources* (Washington, D.C.: The Pastoral Press, 1986).

3. *Epistula Apostolorum* 15, in Edgar Hennecke, *Gospels and Related Writings*, vol. 1 of *New Testament Apocrypha*, ed., R. McL. Wilson (Philadelphia: Westminster Press, 1963) 199.

4. Christine Mohrmann, "Pascha, Passio, Transitus," *Etudes sur le latin des chrétiens* (Rome: Edizioni di storia e letteraturea, 1958) 204-205. [First published in *Ephemerides Liturgicae* 66 (1952) 37-52.]

5. Melito of Sardis, *Paschal Homily*, cited here from A. Hamman, ed., *The Paschal Mystery*, Alba Patristic Library, vol. 3 (Staten Island, NY: Alba House, 1969) 31.

6. Lactantius, *Divine Institutes* 4.26, Ante-Nicene Fathers, vol. 7, 129. For citations of the other texts, cf. Mohrmann, "Pascha" 207-208.

7. Tertullien, *De baptismo* 19.

8. *De pascha computus* 2 (CSEL 3:3).

9. *Homilies on Isaiah* 5.2, cited here in the English of John W. Tyrer, *Historical Survey of Holy Week, Its Services and Ceremonial* (London: Oxford University Press, 1932) 23, where n. 1 supplies the Latin of Jerome.

10. Eusebius, *Ecclesiastical History* V. 24.12.

11. Josef Jungmann, *Pastoral Liturgy* (New York: Herder and Herder, 1962) 105-106. Perhaps the most serious examination of this question is that of Carlo Marcora, *La Vigilia nella liturgia* (Milan, 1954).

12. In Hennecke, *Gospels and Related Writings* 199f.

13. Eusebius, *Ecclesiastical History* V.23.2.

14. Ibid. V.24.

15. Ibid. V.24.14-17.

16. Tyrer, *Historical Survey* 9-10.

17. Although Christmas is still commonly considered an institution native to Rome, some recent studies suggest the possibility that North Africa was this festival's place of origin.

18. Isidore of Seville, *Etymologies* 6.17.10 (PL 82:147).

19. Anton Baumstark, *Comparative Liturgy*, revised by Bernard Botte; English edition by F.L. Cross (London: Mowbray, 1958) 174.

20. Tertullian, *De jejuniis* 14.

21. K. Holl, "Ein Bruchstück aus einem bisher unbekannten Brief des Epiphanius," *Der Osten*, vol. 2 of *Gesammelte Aufsätze zur Kirchege-schichte* (Tübingen: Mohr, 1927) 204-224; M. Richard, "La question pascale au IIe siècle," *L'Orient Syrien* 6 (1961) 179-212.

22. Justin, *First Apology*, chapters 65-67.

23. Mohrmann, "Pascha" 214-216.

24. Gaudentius, *Sermo* 2 (PL 20:858 B); Ambrose, *De sacramentis* I.4.12 (CSEL 73: 20).

25. Dix, *The Shape of the Liturgy* 350

7

The Origin of Lent
at Alexandria

THE OBSERVANCE OF LENT HAS VARIED WIDELY IN CHRISTIAN HISTORY and so has its definition. Given such variety, it is unlikely that we can ever identify a single origin for this major fast of the liturgical year. This chapter will not attempt to address all the evidence, but will concern itself primarily with the season as found in the Byzantine tradition, a pattern which evidences a distinction between Lent itself and Great Week, and which suggests a distinct origin of the fast of forty days rather than an extension of the paschal fast. The hypothesis to be presented is that the fast of forty days had its origin at Alexandria where it followed immediately upon the celebration of Jesus' baptism in Jordan and where it was concluded with the conferral of baptism in a celebration associated with one whom we know as Lazarus.

While writers on the history of Lent, apart from Salaville and Cabié,[1] have tended to claim the phrase *pro tēs tesserakostēs* in canon five of Nicea as the earliest reference to the fast, it has not always proved easy to relate the length of the fast to that of Jesus' temptation in the wilderness, and some have insisted that that identification is only a secondary development. Gregory Dix, for example, wrote of the matter:

> The step of identifying the six weeks' fast with the 40 days' fast of our Lord in the wilderness was obviously in keeping with the new historical interest of the liturgy. The actual number of '40 days' of fasting was made up by extending

87

Lent behind the sixth Sunday before Easter in various ways. But the association with our Lord's fast in the wilderness was an idea attached to the season of Lent only *after* it had come into existence in connnection with the preparation of candidates for baptism.[2]

To this statement, however, he adds a pregnant parenthesis:

(An historical commemoration would strictly have required that Lent should follow immediately upon Epiphany, after this had been accepted as the commemoration of our Lord's baptism.)[3]

Evident in the first part of Dix's statement is his conviction that historical commemoration became a significant factor in liturgical organization only in the fourth century. However, other readings of the evidence have suggested a significant commemorative dimension in the very early observance of pascha by Christians, and some would recognize the second-century accommodation of the paschal celebration to the structure of the week as amounting to that fusion of historical and eschatological factors that Dix assigned only to the fourth century.[4] Where such an accommodation was made, in any case, the one day of the paschal fast became first two days and, by the first half of the third century, the six days reported in *Didascalia Apostolorum*.[5] With the addition of the first four days of the week, the paschal fast achieved its full extent and became that singular week in the year that we know as Holy Week or Great Week, the beginning of which was announced at Alexandria from Dionysius onward,[6] even though the festal letters would come to announce as well the beginning of the fast of forty days.[7]

Byzantine Lent

Whereas western historians have tended to see that forty-day period as a further extension of the one week of the paschal fast to six weeks, Baumstark and others have pointed out that the Byzantine rite reveals a distinction between the fast of forty days and the older paschal fast that amounts to a separation of the two.[8] The forty days are a continuous period from a Monday to the Friday six weeks later, and at vespers on this Friday the *Triodion* includes a text ascribed to Andrew the Blind, a monk of St. Saba in the eighth century:

> Having completed the forty days that bring profit to our soul, let us cry: Rejoice, city of Bethany, home of Lazarus. Rejoice, Martha and Mary, his sisters. Tomorrow Christ will come, by his word to bring your dead brother to life . . .[9]

Here we see both the consummation of the forty days' fast and the transition to the festal Saturday of Lazarus, which, with Palm Sunday, separates that fast from the coming paschal fast. Here Lent has its own conclusion, evidently apart from Easter (although another text at the same vespers will refer to the coming fast of the passion). This distinction between Lent and the paschal fast is even clearer in the medieval Byzantine typika.

Mateos' excellent edition of the Typikon of the Great Church (based on the tenth-century codex 40 of Holy Cross Monastery in Jerusalem with variant readings from the ninth-century codex 266 of the Monastery of St. John on Patmos) gives us a clear picture of the developed Constantinopolitan Lent.[10] It provides for celebrations of the eucharist on all Saturdays and Sundays in Lent. Apart from the first Sunday (now the Feast of Orthodoxy, but in these manuscripts still an independently established feast of the prophets Moses, Aaron, and Samuel),[11] every eucharist has its epistle drawn from Hebrews and its gospel from Mark, series that are, in spite of some displacement on the Saturdays, characteristic of the Constantinopolitan penchant for course reading. The Hebrews series extends to the Saturday of Lazarus, but the gospel on this day is John 11:1-45 (the story of the raising of Lazarus), abandoning the Markan series which had reached to chapter 10, verses 32-45 on the preceding Sunday. This last Markan passage includes Jesus' prediction of his death and resurrection, the request of James and John for places of honor in his kingdom, and Jesus' promise that they shall share in his cup and in his baptism. After the Johannine account of the miracle at Bethany on the final Saturday, it is as well the Johannine version of the entry into Jerusalem that is read on the following Sunday, and all the days of the week leading into that Palm Sunday are called *tōn baiōn*, "of the [palm] branches."

Since the Saturday of Lazarus is but one week before Easter, it is somewhat surprising to discover that it is a fully baptismal liturgy, whose general outline is the same as that for the Epiphany.[12] After orthros, the patriarch goes to the little baptistry and confers baptism and chrismation. A cantor leads the neophytes into the church singing Psalm 31, which he continues till, on a signal from the deacon, the reading of Acts is taken up at the account of the baptism of the Ethiopian eunuch, all this as on the Epiphany. The reading of Acts continues until the beginning of the antiphons of the liturgy. On Lazarus Saturday the first of these is, "By the prayers of the Theotokos," the second, "Alleluia," and the third is the troparion sung previously at orthros, "Giving us before thy Passion an assurance of the general resurrection, thou hast raised Lazarus from the dead, O Christ our God."[13] The Trisagion is replaced by the baptismal troparion, "As many as have been baptized into Christ have put on Christ," a substitution still observed in the Byzantine rite today.[14]

Mateos' tenth-century source (but not that of the ninth) mentions baptism also on the morning of Holy Saturday, and he suggests that both this baptism and that on the Saturday of Lazarus are for the purpose of reducing the numbers of those to be baptized at the paschal vigil.[15] This would be easy to believe of the baptisms on the morning before the vigil where, at the end of orthros, we find the laconic notice: "then, after the dismissal, *ta photismata* are performed by the patriarch in the little baptistry."[16] However, given the absence of this rubric from the Patmos manuscript, prepared for use in a monastery, one is tempted to believe that this was the only occasion for the conferral of baptism at Easter in the tenth century, by which time all such baptisms would be of infants. The more solemn baptismal liturgies, such as that on the Saturday of Lazarus, would be retained in the manuscripts only as textual tradition, continuing evidence of an earlier state of the liturgy.

Still, one may wonder whether there ever was such solemn baptism on this day before Palm Sunday. The baptismal liturgy on the Epiphany related to the theme of that day, the baptism of Jesus. Is there a similar thematic connection between this baptismal day and the raising of Lazarus? Considering its context—a fast of forty days with a course reading of Mark to 10:32-45—I believe there is reason to posit such a connection and I will be concerned to develop this connection, although it would seem to entail assigning a very early date to this Constantinopolitan lenten program.

Pierre-Marie Gy believes that the Sunday gospel readings, at least, were established as early as the second half of the sixth century,[17] but he has established no *terminus post quem*. Is it possible that the main lines of this pattern reach back even earlier? While I believe this to be the case, direct evidence is lacking, so far as I have been able to ascertain.

Chrysostom's *Homily on Psalm 145*[18] was preached on the Saturday of Lazarus and refers to Palm Sunday as well. Although Montfaucon was uncertain as to whether it was delivered in Antioch or Constantinople, it seems clear that it was preached in Constantinople, since Palm Sunday was still viewed as a novelty by Severus at Antioch in the sixth century.[19] Chrysostom's sermon relates both the raising of Lazarus and the entry into Jerusalem to the coming Great Week, although it is clear that there was no procession with palms as at Jerusalem. John 12:17-18 identifies the crowd that went out to meet Jesus upon his entry into Jerusalem with those who had witnessed the raising of Lazarus at Bethany, but apart from this it seems likely that Chrysostom's association of these events in a close juxtaposition not supported by John's chronology reflects their liturgical juxtaposition. We may take it, then, that the Saturday of Lazarus and Palm Sunday immediately preceded Great Week at Constantinople in the time of Chrysostom, and that their gospel readings were from John.

Lazarus Saturday and Palm Sunday at Jerusalem

By the time of the visit of Egeria to Jerusalem (381-384),[20] there is a visit to the Lazarium on the day before Palm Sunday, and this is the earliest clear reference to a commemoration of Lazarus on that day.[21] Still, the Jerusalem evidence is troubling. Dom Cabrol noted long ago that the visit to the Lazarium formed no part of the normal liturgical cursus of Jerusalem.[22] The Friday night vigil reached its conclusion with the Saturday morning eucharist at

Sion and *lucernare* was performed in the Anastasis as usual. It is between these services and at an hour of no particular liturgical significance (one o'clock in the afternoon) that the visit to the Lazarium takes place. There is a preliminary assembly about half a mile from the Lazarium itself, and the pilgrim tells us that it was here that Mary met Jesus. In like manner, the monks meet the bishop, and all enter the church where, says Egeria, "they have one hymn and an antiphon, and a reading from the Gospel about Lazarus' sister meeting the Lord."[23] After a prayer and a blessing, the procession moves on to the tomb of Lazarus where, in Egeria's favorite but here puzzling phrase, "they have hymns and antiphons which—like all the readings—are suitable to the day and the place."[24] Why suitable to the day? What is the connection between the raising of Lazarus and the Saturday before Great Week? Egeria offers no help here, not even to the extent of telling us which lessons are read at the Lazarium. She does add, however, that at the dismissal a presbyter announces the pascha. "He mounts a platform," she says, "and reads the Gospel passage which begins, 'When Jesus came to Bethany six days before the Passover.'" She adds, "They do it on this day because the Gospel describes what took place in Bethany 'six days before the Passover,' and it is six days from this Saturday to the Thursday night on which the Lord was arrested after the Supper."[25] This gospel, John 12, as we shall see shortly, considerably confuses the nature of this observance.

While the possibility of another gospel prior to this at the dismissal cannot be excluded for the time of Egeria, the Armenian lectionary of the following century is specific.[26] The initial gathering where Lazarus' sister encountered Jesus has disappeared. The title assigned for the assembly makes no reference to Lazarus himself (beyond assigning the Lazarium as the station), but is simply: "The sixth day before the Pasch of the Law, Saturday."[27] Still, Psalm 29 is sung with verse 4 as antiphon [Heb. Ps 30:3]: "You brought up my soul, O Lord, from Hades..." The epistle is 1 Thess 4:13-18: "Brethren, I would not have you ignorant concerning those who are asleep..." The Alleluia has Psalm 39 [40] whose opening verses are again appropriate to the raising of Lazarus. While all these appointments are given for the Saturday before Palm Sunday, they appear as well on the sixth day of the Epiphany octave, also at the Lazarium, where they are followed by the gospel account of Lazarus' resurrection, John 11:1-46.[28] Here on the Saturday before Palm Sunday, however, this gospel is not read, but rather that which Egeria characterized as the announcement of pascha, John 11:55-12:11,[29] and this seems very curious. The gospel comes as the climax of a canon that is clearly concerned with the raising of Lazarus, even without the earlier gathering at the place of Jesus' encounter with Lazarus' sister. But just when this series of texts reaches its climax, the reading of the gospel, there is an abrupt change of subject. After the phrase, "Six days before the Passover," this pericope describes an entirely distinct and subsequent visit of Jesus to Bethany, the last visit during which Mary anointed him. This story was also in the Jerusalem lectionary in the version of Matthew on Wednesday of Great Week (Matthew placing it "two days before the Passover").[30] The duplication of the story can be seen in the earliest stratum of the Armenian lectionary (Jerusalem 121), but the slightly later Paris manuscript (*arm.* 44), sensitive to the duplication, reduces the gospel for Wednesday of Great Week to only three verses so as to remove the redundancy.[31]

Clearly, however, it was this Matthean chronology that was primary for Jerusalem, since only a synoptic source could identify Thursday night as "the Passover of the Law." For the Fourth Gospel, Passover fell in the night from Friday to Saturday. Therefore, the use of a Johannine text to announce the Passover of the Law on the night before the crucifixion betrays a secondary development.

However we reconstruct the synaxis at the Lazarium sketchily reported by Egeria, it is clear that then, and still in the time represented by the Armenian lectionary, there is a special synaxis, which, while it sets out as celebration of the raising of Lazarus, is yet concerned to turn this observance back toward the onset of the coming fast of the passion. Michel Aubineau, the editor of the homilies of Hesychius of Jerusalem, observes of this Saturday before Palm Sunday: "it seems indeed that the liturgical feast of the Saturday was oriented rather toward the proximate 'Great Week,' toward Pascha and the Passion of the Lord."[32] It is difficult to avoid the suspicion that someone in Jerusalem was asking what the raising of Lazarus has to do with this Saturday before Great Week. But if the focus of the observance was so uncertain, why have it at all? One very attractive possibility is that it was to satisfy the desires of pilgrims to the Holy City who already knew this as an important day in the liturgical life of their local church and wished to visit on this day the site of the miracle it commemorated. Nonetheless, by the time of Egeria a special gospel at the dismissal turns the observance toward the coming paschal fast, and in the following century this became the gospel of the day, relating Bethany and Lazarus to the coming passion. In the later Georgian versions of the Jerusalem lectionary from the fifth to the eighth centuries, the epistle, too, is changed from that chosen for the celebration of Lazarus' resurrection to one oriented more toward the coming week, Ephesians 5:13-17: "Look carefully then how you walk, not as unwise men but as wise, making the most of the time, because the days are evil."[33]

By this time, surely, Constantinople had its course reading of Hebrews extending through Lent and the Saturday of Lazarus, suggesting that the latter day is the festal conclusion of the forty days' fast, not an incidental day unrelated to Lent. Then, however, remembering the Markan lenten course reading that gives way abruptly to John's account of the miracle at Bethany, one is impelled to ask what the raising of Lazarus has to do with such a Lent, and even what it has to do with baptism.

In any case, the differences we noted between the Saturday of Lazarus at Jerusalem and the picture available later at Constantinople do not suggest that the Jerusalem rite is the source of the Constantinopolitan. Still, it seems unlikely that this lenten program was native to Constantinople. The small port city of Byzantium, suffragan to the see of Heraclea, was radically transformed by being made the seat of empire from 324 (and formally from 330). If there is reason to believe that this Constantinopolitan lenten program did not derive from Jerusalem, was it then taken over from another of the ancient sees, and if so, which?

Antioch contributed significantly to the liturgical traditions of Cappadocia, Asia Minor, and Constantinople, but our information on the organization of Lent there in the fourth century is limited to *Apostolic Constitutions*. Chapter 13 of the fifth book gives a picture that could well be consistent with the later pattern at Constantinople: the fast of forty days begins on Monday and ends on Friday, though the number of weeks is not specified. The fast is then broken off until the paschal fast begins on the following Monday. We should see this, surely, as such a six week fast as we find at Costantinople, although the passage (a general view of the feasts and fasts) suggests no particular liturgical observance related to the Saturday and Sunday between the six-week fast and the paschal fast. Burkitt edited a somewhat later Syriac lectionary of the late fifth or early sixth century. However, this document, which Burkitt assigned to an area outside Antioch, shows a very different organization. Here liturgical provision is made for only the first and middle weeks of Lent, each beginning on a Sunday.[34] The Sunday that introduces the middle week has as its gospel John 11:1-44, but two alternatives are provided, Luke 7:11-17 (the raising of the son of the widow of Nain) or Mark 5:21-43 (the raising of the daughter of Jairus). No provisions are made for the week preceding Great Week, but those for the Sunday that opens Great Week reach back to Saturday night where, after the evening service, there is a reading of John 12:1-11 (the anointing at Bethany, "six days before the Passover").[35] Such an arrangement would be consistent with the testimony of Socrates concerning those who begin their fast seven weeks before Easter, but fast only three five-day periods.[36] At Antioch itself in the sixth century, Severus speaks of a continuous fast of eight weeks yielding forty days of fasting, and (as noted above) he regards Palm Sunday as a novelty.[37] It should also be noted that we do not find at Antioch the strong predilection for course reading that we see in the Byzantine liturgy. In sum, in spite of the similarity between the pattern of the fasts in *Apostolic Constitutions* V.13 and that at Constantinople (a pattern shared as well at Jerusalem in the Armenian lectionary), there is no clear sign of an Antiochene source for the content of the lenten liturgy found at Constantinople.

Lent at Alexandria

As for Alexandria, the other and perhaps the greatest of the ancient sees of the Eastern Church, there is a tempting coincidence: three of the four Markan gospels for the Sundays in Lent at Constantinople are integral Coptic chapters according to the divisions noted by Horner in his edition of the Bohairic New Testament.[38] None of these finds a place in the Coptic lenten appointments according to the late and admittedly defective Qatamarus (lectionary) translated by Malan,[39] and of the three only one finds a place at any point in the year. These divisions, then, do not seem to reflect an influence of Constantinople on the Coptic manuscripts. Of the three that are Coptic chapters, one also corresponds to a Greek chapter. Otherwise, none of the Byzantine lenten gospels corresponds to a chapter in the Greek manuscripts.

While such a coincidence might tempt us to suspect an early Egyptian influence on the Byzantine lenten liturgy, from the time of Athanasius and for centuries after him Lent at Alexandria is quite different from that of Constantinople. Current Coptic usage is not unlike the Byzantine, being divided into three periods: a week of forefast (kept with the same stringency as the other weeks, unlike the mitigated fast of the Byzantine tyrophagy), then the six weeks of Lent ending in the Saturday of Lazarus and Palm Sunday (this latter one of seven principal feasts), and finally the week of the paschal fast.[40] This similarity, however, is largely the result of Byzantine influence since the tenth century (or perhaps earlier), and Rahlfs argued that behind this lay a fast of eight weeks intended to yield forty days of actual fasting, such a practice as was just mentioned in connection with Severus at Antioch and was also reported for Jerusalem by Egeria.[41] This eight-week fast can first be seen at Alexandria in fragments of festal letters of Benjamin I, patriarch from 622 to 661.[42] Earlier than this, and as late as 577,[43] Alexandria had the six week fast before Easter first promulgated there by Athanasius in his second festal letter for 330.[44] While the paschal fast was included as the final week of this longer fast, the separate indication of the beginning of the paschal fast in all the festal letters that announce the fast of forty days (whether over six weeks or eight) testifies to the prior existence of that six-day fast, visible at Alexandria as early as the patriarchate of Dionysius (247-ca. 264). In none of this can one see any background for the Constantinopolitan Lent, six weeks distinct from the paschal fast and separated from it by the Saturday of Lazarus and Palm Sunday.

In this present century, however, several scholars have pointed to a persistent, if late, Coptic tradition asserting that until the patriarchate of Demetrius (189-ca. 232) the fast of forty days was begun on the day following the Epiphany, the commemoration of Christ's baptism in Jordan, just such a strict historical commemoration as that which Dix denied. While this tradition has been discussed by Louis Villecourt,[45] Anton Baumstark,[46] and Jean-Michel Hanssens,[47] it is René Coquin who has given it its most careful and critical scrutiny.[48] Tracing the assertion of a forty-day fast following the Epiphany from its *locus classicus* in *The Lamp of Darkness* (a Coptic Church encyclopedia by the fourteenth-century scholar, Abu 'l-Barakat),[49] through the *Synaxarium Alexandrinum* (given its final redaction by Michael of Malig in the first half of the thirteenth century),[50] to the *Annals* of Eutychius (the tenth-century Melchite patriarch of Alexandria),[51] Coquin argues that Eutychius or his source confused two matters: the establishment of the computation for the date of Easter (in which Demetrius probably was involved),[52] and the separate matter of the translation of the fast of forty days from its place after Epiphany to its familiar position prior to Easter. This latter change Coquin at first took to be a personal initiative of Athanasius,[53] but in a subsequent paper he presented literary evidence for the settlement of the time of the fast together with the paschal date by the Council of Nicea.[54]

Alexandria's Baptismal Day

Somewhat more problematic than the assertion that there was such a primitive forty day fast following Epiphany is the further suggestion that this fast was terminated with the conferral of baptism on the Friday of the sixth week.[55] Conybeare had reported a similar assertion of a post-Epiphany quadragesima for the first 120 years of the church's life from a twelfth- century Armenian document ascribed to Isaac Catholicos (Sahag), but Conybeare supposed that this fast followed after the communal celebration of baptism on Epiphany.[56] Whatever is to be made of this Armenian testimony, nothing in Conybeare's treatment of it suggests that the fast of which it speaks ended in the conferral of baptism. The source that identifies the "Friday of the sixth week of the blessed fast" as the traditional Coptic baptismal day is a letter of the tenth-century Bishop of Memphis, Macarius;[57] but he makes no reference to the fast falling after Epiphany. Several writers have referred to Macarius' letter and have understood his "Friday of the sixth week" to refer to one or other of the last three Fridays before Easter, as they understood the prepaschal fast at Alexandria to consist of six,[58] seven,[59] or eight[60] weeks. Coquin, however, seems to suppose that Macarius refers rather to the conclusion of the primitive fast after Epiphany. This, of course, was no longer the position of the major fast in the tenth century, and Macarius does not refer to the fast falling after Epiphany. Nonetheless, Macarius shows himself to be an extremely conservative defender of what he takes to be a usage of greatest antiquity, and it is quite possible that his reference to baptism on the sixth day of the sixth week of the fast should be understood as a dimension of the conclusion of the fast of forty days, whatever its position relative to Epiphany or Easter. This day, known as "the seal of the fast," is still the occasion of a general anointing of the sick, Qandil.[61]

Macarius' concern is to complain of the accommodation of ancient Coptic tradition to Byzantine practice in the matter of the consecration of chrism. He describes the Coptic rite in great detail, noting various changes in practice over the years. After describing the performance of the rite in Alexandria's Church of the Evangelists, for example, he says that it was done later only at the Monastery of Macarius in the desert of Scete after, as he puts it, "the confusion and disturbance had overcome us," probably a reference to the establishment of a Melchite patriarchate following the Council of Chalcedon. By this time other changes had already diminished the impressiveness of the day's functions and, he says, "it was not complete." There were no longer baptisms on the day nor any scrutiny on the preceding Wednesday. All that remained of the original Alexandrian custom was the consecration of the chrism, and now, at the request of some secretaries and archontes who wished to be present, this had been delayed until the Thursday of Great Week, an accommodation to Greek custom that became final in the patriarchate of Ephrem the Syrian in 970.[62] In contrast to this practice, he tells us that "our rule is to make the chrism on the day of Friday of the sixth week of the blessed fast, because of the baptism according to the custom which was current in the beginning. This rite was performed in the city of Alexandria, see of Mari Mark the Evangelist." [63] The baptism included the anointing of the neophytes with the newly consecrated chrism, followed by the celebration of eucharist and the giving of milk and honey. But by his own time only the consecration of the chrism remained to mark the importance of the day, and now this had been surrendered. Macarius laments:

> It was thus that there was introduced a custom to please the people and the rule of the see of Mark the Evangelist was changed. They knew not that touching this day, and on it, there were numerous virtues, mysteries and interpretations. And this because it is the consummation of the sacred quarantine and is the day of the fast. It is told that *this is the day on which the Lord Christ baptized his disciples*. This is the sixth day of the week, figure of the sixth millenary, on which God the Word was incarnate and delivered Adam and his posterity from the domination of the enemy over them and freed them from his enslavement. And it became the day of baptism. This is why the patriarch of Alexandria performed on it the consecration of the chrism, which is the oil of balm, and the oil of gladness, which is the oil of olive, and of the water of baptism, and he baptized then the people of every land. [64]

From this it is clear that Macarius considered the abandoned day to be a very ancient focus of Alexandrian tradition. The suggestion that it was the consummation of a primitive fast after Epiphany receives support from the story of an encounter between Theophilus, Patriarch of Alexandria from 385 to 412, and Orsisius, hegoumen of Tabennis and third abbot general of the Pachomian monasteries. While this account appears in Arabic in the tenth-century *History of the Patriarchs of Alexandria* by Severus of El-Asmounein, [65] the more detailed form of the story is in a Coptic papyrus codex of the sixth or seventh century formerly in the Phillipps Library in Cheltenham. [66] The account there begins with a letter from Theophilus to Orsisius bidding him to come to Alexandria. Although the letter does not explain fully, it becomes clear that this was in consequence of a disturbing experience at the consecration of the baptismal font on what Theophilus calls, "the appropriate day." (The Arabic version speaks of "the week of baptisms.") The letter was dispatched at the hands of two deacons, Faustus and Timotheus, and they, having finally located Orsisius in the south, brought him back to Alexandria. After an exchange of compliments between the hegoumen and the patriarch, the account relates of Theophilus:

> After this he declared to him the mystery, namely: from time immemorial when my Fathers came to confer baptism on the appropriate day there used to come, as they prayed still at the font, a beam of light and sign the waters. However, in this year we were not worthy of seeing this; and since I was frightened and upset, I revealed the matter to the clergy. And in the night of Saturday I went to present the oblation, and I heard a voice out of the sanctuary which said, "If Orsisius does not come, you will not see that which you desire."[67]

Theophilus concludes his address by asking Orsisius to come with him to the church where waits the Christ who has called for him, and they arrive there, according to the text, "on the great parasceve of the Great Pascha, early in the morning on the sabbath." Theophilus opens the baptistry and begins the consecration. The prodigy occurs as formerly, now that Orsisius is included in the ceremony. After the baptisms, early in the morning of Easter Sunday, they proceed to the Catholikon (cathedral) for the liturgy. "In this wise," says the author of the account, "the feast was doubled: the Resurrection and the baptism; and thus it is done until this day."[68]

From this narrative, whose fundamental historicity was defended by Ehrhard in a *Beitrag* appended to Crum's edition of the text,[69] it is quite clear that until this meeting between Theophilus and Orsisius the "appropriate day" for baptism was well prior to Easter. We are not told precisely what that day was, but it would seem that the search for Orsisius was not a simple one. According to the codex, Timotheus and Faustus searched for him from community to community and their quest is referred to as a wandering. Once they had found him, according to the account, the return to Alexandria was accomplished by boat in six days, although Crum questioned the possibility of making a trip of between 550 and 800 kilometers with such speed.[70] In any case, the "appropriate day" for baptism on which the prodigy failed to occur must have been some weeks prior to Orsisius' arrival at Alexandria on Saturday of Holy Week. This would be consistent with a baptismal day in the final week of a six week fast following Epiphany, a structure that remained in place in spite of Athanasius' attempts to promulgate the forty day fast before Easter.

The scant information yielded by Severus' *History of the Patriarchs of Alexandria* is consistent with such a reconstruction. This tenth-century document, an Alexandrian equivalent to the Roman *Liber Pontificalis*, presents many of the same problems of historical reliability for the early biographies as does that Latin document. The author, however, seems aware of the problem and is careful to inform the reader of his sources and even to name the assistants who participated in the translations from Coptic and Greek.[71] Typical of this relatively sophisticated historiography is the presentation of two significantly variant accounts of the martyrdom of Peter I, patriarch from 300 to 311. As background to Peter's martyrdom, the biography relates a story of a woman of Antioch who brought her children to Alexandria to be baptized, arriving there, the account says, "in the week of Baptism, which is the sixth week of the Fast, when infants are baptized . . ."[72] No further information is given on the situation of this fast in the year, but the following biographies of Alexander and Athanasius both assign the establishment of the time of the fast as well as that of the date of Easter to the Council of Nicea.[73] Such an ascription of the establishment of the time of the fast to the council poses the question of whether Severus was aware that the six-week fast mentioned in the earlier biography of Peter I was separate from Easter. Certainly his account of the patriarchate of Demetrius makes no mention of the transfer of the fast from after Epiphany to before Easter, as does the treatment of Demetrius in the *Annals* of the Melchite patriarch, Eutychius, whom Evetts describes as a rival historian whom Severus is often concerned to refute.[74] However that may be, nothing in the *History of the Patriarchs* is inconsistent with Coquin's reconstruction, and it testifies that prior to Nicea (specifically, in the time of Peter I at the opening of the fourth century), the traditional time for baptism was already the sixth week of the fast. Severus also supports Coquin's later suggestion that the fixing of the fast before Pascha was a dimension of the settlement of the paschal question at Nicea.[75]

The Day on Which Christ Baptized

Perhaps the most curious statement made by Macarius is that the Friday of that sixth week was said to be the day on which Jesus baptized his disciples. Four centuries later, Abu 'l-Barakat tells us that the week before the paschal fast ends with the Saturday of Lazarus and the feast of Palms on the seventh Sunday. This feast of Palms he describes as the end of the holy quarantine, adding that formerly (until the time of Demetrius) this was the pasch of the fast after Epiphany, the Pascha of the Resurrection being then observed at its own time in the month of Nisan.[76] Of the preceding sixth Sunday of the fast, he says that it is called the Sunday of the baptism(s), that it is the day on which the chrism was prepared, and that it was said that the baptism of the apostles took place then.[77] Since the preparation of the chrism was definitely on Thursday of Great Week by his time, he is here (as in his discussion of Palm Sunday) only relating past lore, translated into the prepaschal Lent of his own day. It is nonetheless interesting that he says of the sixth Sunday just what Macarius said of the Friday six days later, that it had baptismal significance based on a tradition associating the day with the performance of baptism by Jesus. Of this association, Coquin wrote:

> We have not been able to discover the source of that Coptic tradition touching the baptism of the Apostles after the temptation in the desert, but it is evident that the Coptic Church primitively adopted an organization of that part of the liturgical year calculated on the historical unfolding of the life of Jesus, at least as that was given in its own traditions.[78]

This statement of the problem regarding the source of this tradition needs, I believe, two amendments. First, while Abu 'l-Barakat does refer to the baptism of the *apostles*, the earlier letter of Macarius speaks rather of the baptism of *disciples*, and this seems preferable. Second, this day is never spoken of as coming at the conclusion of Jesus' fast, but rather at the conclusion of the church's imitation of that fast. Any literary account of Jesus' temptation would be rather brief, but the church's observance of these forty days really takes forty days, a period during which one would not expect the suspension of further reference to the life of Jesus. Such reference to Jesus' baptism of disciples, then, would be found at whatever point the unfolding of the local tradition of his life had reached by the end of the forty days of the church's fasting. The tradition would not seem to be one of the Gospels, since only John makes any reference to baptism by Jesus, and that severely restricted if not reworked; but John gives no account of the temptation in the wilderness. This story, so critical for the fast, is found only in the synoptics, and they contain no reference to baptism by Jesus.

Such, at least, was the impasse at which assessment of this Coptic tradition seemed to have arrived until the publication in 1973 of Professor Morton Smith's exhaustive study of the manuscript that he had found in 1958 at the Monastery of Mar Saba near Jerusalem.[79] This fragment (in a Greek cursive of the eighteenth century, copied into the end of a seventeenth-century printed edition of the epistles of Ignatius of Antioch) purports to be a copy of a letter of Clement of Alexandria to a certain Theodore, congratulating him on silencing the Carpocratians and correcting certain misconceptions planted by them regarding a *mystikon evaggelion*, a secret gospel of Mark possessed by the Church of Alexandria. This letter has been subjected to extensive examination by a large number of biblical and patristic scholars, and the general view today seems to support Smith's finding that the letter is indeed by Clement.[80] Of the secret gospel, Clement says that it was written by Mark at Alexandria as an expansion of what he had written at Rome for the use of catechumens, "selecting what he thought most useful for increasing the faith of those who were being instructed."[81] In contrast to the earlier version, he describes the expanded text as "a more spiritual gospel for the use of those who were being perfected," in which, "to the stories already written he added yet others, and moreover, brought in certain sayings of which he knew the interpretation would, as a mystagogue, lead the hearers into the innermost sanctuary of that truth hidden by seven veils."[82] Clement continues, "dying, he left this composition to the Church in Alexandria, where it is even yet most carefully guarded, being read only to those who are being initated into the great mysteries."[83]

The letter gives two quotations from this secret gospel, a brief addition to Mark 10:46 and, more significant to our present concern, a long addition following Mark 10:34. Clement writes to Theodore:

> To you, therefore, I shall not hesitate to answer the questions you have asked, refuting the falsifications by the very words of the Gospel. For example, after "and they were in the road going to Jerusalem," and what follows, until "After three days he shall rise," [Mark 10.32-34] the secret Gospel brings the following material word for word: "And they come into Bethany. And a certain woman whose brother had died was there. And, coming, she prostrated herself before Jesus and says to him, "Son of David, have mercy on me." But the disciples rebuked her. And Jesus, being angered, went off with her into the garden where the tomb was, and straightway a great cry was heard from the tomb. And going in where the youth was, he stretched forth his hand and raised him, seizing his hand. But the youth, looking upon him, loved him and began to beseech him that he might be with him. And going out of the tomb they came into the house of the youth, for he was rich. And *after six days* Jesus told him what to do and in the evening the youth comes to him, wearing a linen cloth over his naked body. And he remained with him that night, for Jesus taught him the mystery of the kingdom of God. And thence, arising, he returned to the other side of the Jordan." After these words follows the text "And James and John come to him," [Mark 10.35] and all that section.[84]

The section to which Clement refers, of course, includes Jesus' promise to James and John that they shall share in his cup and in his baptism, concluding, "For the Son of man came not to be served but to serve, and to give his life as a ransom for many." This passage (Mark 10:35-45), together with the three verses cited by Clement to introduce this Bethany story (Mark 10:32-34), constitutes chapter 31 in the Coptic numbering, and is the pericope that serves as the gospel for the fifth Sunday of Lent at Constantinople at the eucharist next before that on the Saturday of Lazarus. On this Saturday, "memorial of the holy and just Lazarus," John 11:1-45 supplies the only canonical version of the story of the miracle at Bethany recounted in the secret gospel of Mark and is, I believe, a surrogate for it.

Whatever may have been the origin of the secret pericope, it is clear that Clement regards it as related to initiation in its use in the Church at Alexandria, observing that it is read only to the candidates. This is borne out in its content as well by the nocturnal meeting of the young man with Jesus in a special costume that would facilitate disrobing for and dressing after whatever ceremony of washing or anointing. This initiatory reference is borne out also by its context, just prior to Jesus' promise to James and John that they shall share in his cup and in his baptism. This location within the gospel, however, is not at the conclusion of its account of Jesus' temptation in the wilderness, but at a point which we can recognize as the conclusion of a six-week course reading during the church's imitation of Jesus' fast, a reading which began with the account of Jesus' baptism in Jordan, "The beginning of the gospel of Jesus Christ," on 6 January. This, we now know, was a date that Clement associated with the birth of Christ.[85] But whether from the time of Clement or from later in the third century, the passage seems likely to have been that for the old baptismal day in the sixth week of the fast. Standardization of gospel texts would force the suppression of such a peculiar local tradition, but not before that story had become so established within the tradition that its suppression would bring the substitution of the only canonical parallel, the Johannine account of the raising of Lazarus.

Alexandria's Lenten Program at Constantinople

The connection of the fast of forty days with the baptism of Jesus would be largely neutralized as Christological development placed emphasis on the nativity rather than on the baptism as the beginning of the gospel. This, together with growing emphasis on Easter baptism, would bring about the dissolution of this old Alexandrian pattern: the celebration of Jesus' baptism (not as isolated event, but as "the beginning of the gospel" in the gospel of the church of Mark the evangelist), then the imitative observance of his forty days' fast (while the gospel continued to unfold), and at the end of the fast the celebration of the rites of initiation, including the tradition of the secret gospel of Mark with its story of the resurrection and initiation of Jesus' disciple at Bethany. The entire season concluded with the celebration of the feast of palms, celebrating Christ's entry into Jerusalem (Mark 11).

The process of dissolving this pattern began with the attempted transposition of the fast by Athanasius after Nicea, an evidently unpopular initiative that he first took in 330 but for which he was still contending a decade later, as can be seen in the letter to Serapion, which accompanied the festal letter of 340.[86] But about the same period, I would suggest, the forming liturgical organization at Constantiople found a way to give a new home to this venerable Alexandrian liturgical pattern, as it did to so much else that was venerable in the more ancient sees of the eastern part of the empire. There, apart from its situation just prior to the paschal fast, Constantinople perpetuated the old Alexandrian tradition: the reading of the Gospel of Mark during the fast of forty days to Mark 10.32-45, then the concluding baptismal day with its account of the raising from the dead of the youth of Bethany, now in its Johannine form.

Constantinopolitan visitors to Jerusalem accustomed to the Saturday of Lazarus would find a visit to the tomb of this disciple at Bethany appropriate, and could be expected to make their desires known. It is otherwise difficult to relate this miracle to the Saturday before the paschal fast. Indeed, noting that the putatively Markan version of that story stands in this Gospel close to the Markan account of the entry into Jerusalem (Mark 11), an account which is itself unrelated to Mark's passion narrative, one is prompted to ask whether Constantinople's Johannine account of the entry, which does relate this event to the passion chronology, is not also a substitution for a Markan original. Abu 'l-Barakat, we have noted, did say that in primitive Alexandrian use, the feast of Palms "was formerly the pasch of the Fast, that, and not the Pascha of the Resurrection, when the holy quarantine began its fast on the twelfth of Tybi . . . and the week of the

Pascha was celebrated apart in the month of Nisan . . ."[87] In such a case, what we have suggested of the visit to the Lazarium in Jerusalem described by Egeria might also be true for the very similar assembly on the Mount of Olives on the following day. The Jerusalem re-enactment with an actual procession with palms, that is to say, may have been the Holy City's only contribution to an already established celebration of the entry of Christ into Jerusalem, a celebration whose connection to the preceding celebration of the miracle at Bethany is clearer in the secret gospel of Mark than it is in the Johannine equivalents at Constantinople. John provides no close chronological connection between the two events, yet the Saturday of Lazarus at Constantinople is still known in the typika of the ninth and tenth centuries as "Saturday of the Palm-bearer, memorial of the holy and just Lazarus."

Elsewhere, and from a very early period, paschal baptism would demand other arrangements for the final catechetical and exorcistic exercises on behalf of the elect, perhaps even the three weeks at Rome remembered by Socrates.[88] Such baptismal preparation, however, is not to be set over against the imitation of the fast of Jesus as origin of the fast of forty days. Lent in primitive Alexandria was both strict historical commemoration of the fast of Jesus and a time of preparation for baptism. It remained both of these when, after the Council of Nicea, the end of the forty days fell just prior to the paschal fast, encouraging us to see Lent as preparation for Easter.[89] It is sure that preparation for Easter had already included some period prior to the paschal fast in churches that baptized at Easter. Alexandria, however, was not (and is not today) one of these churches.[90]

While the Coptic Lent has now been conformed to the common oriental pattern, I would argue that from its ante-Nicene roots it gave to the rest of the church the notion of a baptismal preparation imitative of the fast of Jesus in the wilderness, the conferral of baptism associated with Jesus' raising from the dead of a disciple at Bethany, and the conclusion of this formative season with the celebration of Christ's entry into Jerusalem, all independent of Easter. If this argument can be sustained, perhaps its most astonishing implication is that the liturgical employment of the primitive but long forgotten Alexandrian expansion of the Gospel of Mark, described in the Mar Saba Clementine fragment, has been known to us all along in the Byzantine celebration of the Saturday of Lazarus, with its odd displacement of the Trisagion by the baptismal troparion, "As many as have been baptized into Christ have put on Christ." So liturgical tradition harbors our history, even when we have lost sight of it.

Notes

1. S. Salaville, "La Tesserakostê au Ve canon de Nicée," *Echos d'Orient*13 (1910) 65-72; 14 (1911) 355-357; R. Cabié, *La Pentecôte* (Tournai: Desclée, 1965) 183-185.

2. Gregory Dix, *The Shape of the Liturgy* (London: Dacre, 1945) 354.

3. Ibid. 354f.

4. This was examined further in chapter 6 of this volume, "History and Eschatology in the Primitive Pascha." Cf. also Robert Taft, S.J., "Historicism Revisited," *Beyond East and West: Problems in Liturgical Understanding*, NPM Studies in Church Music and Liturgy (Washington, D.C.: The Pastoral Press, 1984) 15-30.

5. R.H. Connolly, *Didascalia Apostolorum* (Oxford: Clarendon Press, 1929) 189. The commemorative dimension is particuarly clear here, with each day being assigned to some event in the passion chronology.

6. C.L. Feltoe, *Dionysiou Leipsana: The Letters and Other Remains of Dionysius of Alexandria* (Cambridge: Cambridge University Press, 1904) 101f.

7. *The Festal Letters of S. Athanasius* (Oxford, 1854) 21. This second festal letter of Athanasius, issued for 330, is the first to announce the fast of forty days; it is also our earliest testimony to the exact duration of a fast of that title.

8. Anton Baumstark, *Comparative Liturgy* (Oxford: Mowbray, 1957) 195f.; A. Rahlfs, "Die alttestamentlichen Lektionen der grieschische Kirche," *Nachrichten der K. Gesellschaft der Wissenschaften zu Göttingen. Philologisch-historische Klasse* (1915) 100.

9. Mother Mary and Archimandrite Kallistos Ware, trans., *The Lenten Triodion* (London and Boston: Faber and Faber, 1978) 465f.

10. Juan Mateos, *Le Typicon de la Grande Eglise: Ms. Sainte-Croix no. 40, Xe siècle*, 2 vols., Orientalia Christiana Analecta, vols. 165, 166 (Rome: Pontificio Istituto Orientale, 1962, 1963).

11. Ibid., vol. 1, xii-xiv. For the description of the lenten services, cf. vol. 2, 11-65.

12. Ibid., vol. 2, 62-65; cf. vol. 1, 184-187.

13. Ibid., vol. 2, 62-63.

14. Ibid. 64-65.

15. Ibid. 63, n. 2.

16. Ibid. 84-85.

17. P.-M. Gy, "La Question du système des lectures de la liturgie Byzantine," *Miscellanea Liturgica in onore di sua eminenza il cardinale Giacomo Lercaro*, vol. 2 (Rome, 1967) 251-261.

18. PG 55:519ff.

19. Sermon 125 (PO 29:247-249).

20. For the dating, cf. Paul Devos, "La date du voyage d'Egerie," *Analecta Bollandiana* 85 (1967) 165-184.

21. *Peregrinatio Egeriae* 29.3-6.

22. DACL 82:2087. However, he believed the visit to be native to Jerusalem.

23. The translation is that of John Wilkinson, *Egeria's Travels* (London: S.P.C.K., 1971) 131. [Standard reference, 29.4.]

24. Ibid. 132 [29.5]

25. Ibid. [29.6]

26. Athanase Renoux, *Le Codex Arménien Jérusalem 121*, vol. 2, *Edition comparee du texte et de deux autres manuscrits*, PO 36, fasc. 2 (Turnhout, 1971) 255 [117].

27. Ibid.

28. Ibid. 221 [83].

29. Ibid. 257 [119].

30. Ibid. 265 [127]. The phrase "two days before the Passover" (Mt 26:2) comes at the conclusion of the reading for Tuesday.

31. Ibid. note 3.

32. Michel Aubineau, *Les Homélies festales d'Hésychius de Jérusalem*, Subsidia Hagiographica, vol. 59 (Brussels: Société des Bollandistes, 1978) 388. Renoux says that this function at the Lazarium in the account of Egeria has only the purpose of relating the coming of Jesus to Bethany, six days before Pascha. [*Le Codex Arménien Jérusalem 121*, I, 78]

33. M. Tarchnischvili, ed., *Le Grand lectionnaire de l'Eglise de Jérusalem (Ve-VIIIe siècle)*, CSCO 189 (Louvain, 1959) 81.

34. F.C. Burkitt, *The Early Syriac Lectionary System*, From the Proceedings of the British Academy, vol. 2 (London: Oxford University Press, 1923) 6-7.

35. Ibid.

36. *Ecclesiastical History* V.22.

37. Rahlfs, "Die Alttestamentlichen Lektionen" 100-101; cf. n. 19 above.

38. G. Horner, *The Coptic Version of the New Testament in the Northern Dialect* (Oxford, 1889). For an explanation of the indications of the Coptic "smaller chapters" and the Greek "larger chapters," see his

introduction, pp. xiiif. A convenient table of the Greek and Coptic chapters compared with modern designations and the Ammonian sections will be found in L. Villecourt, ed., *Livre de la lampe des ténèbres*, PO 20, fasc. 4 (Paris, 1928) 34-43.

39. Smith and Cheethan, *A Dictionary of Christian Antiquities*, vol. 2 (Hartford, 1880) 960.

40. O.H.E. Khs-Burmester, *The Egyptian or Coptic Church* (Cairo: French Institute of Oriental Archeology, 1967) 13.

41. Egeria, 27.1 [p. 128 in Wilkinson, *Egeria's Travels*].

42. Rahlfs, "Die alttestamentlichen Lektionen" 85ff.

43. Ibid. 84.

44. Cf. n. 7 above.

45. L. Villecourt, Un manuscrit arabe sur le saint chrême dans l'Eglise copte," *Revue d'histoire ecclésiastique* 18 (1922) 17f.

46. Baumstark, *Comparative Liturgy* 194.

47. J.-M. Hanssens, *La Liturgie d'Hippolyte: Documents et études*, Orientalia Christiana Analecta, vol. 155 (Rome: Pontificio Istituto Orientale, 1959) 449.

48. René-Georges Coquin, "Les origines de l'Epiphanie en Egypte," *Nöel-Epiphanie: Retour du Christ*, Lex Orandi, vol. 40 (Paris 1967) 139ff.

49. There is as yet no complete version of this work in a western language. For the material concerning the fasts we must rely on the French version of Dom Louis Villecourt, "Les observances liturgiques et la discipline du jeûne dans l'Eglise copte. IV: Jeûnes et Semaine-Sainte," *Le Muséon* 38 (1925) 261-330.

50. J. Forget, trans., *Synaxarium Alexandrinum*, CSCO, Arab. 18 (Rome, 1921) 64f., 111f.

51. PG 111.989.

52. Cf. Marcel Richard, "Le Comput pascal par Octaéteris," *Le Muséon* 87 (1974) 307-339.

53. Coquin, "Les origines" 148-154.

54. R.G. Coquin, "Une reforme liturgique du concile de Nicee (325)?," *Comptes Rendus, Académie des Inscriptions et Belles-Lettres* (Paris, 1967). The sources cited are late (ninth or tenth century), but what they assert is consistent with the appearance of the prepaschal Lent only after the council. Particularly impressive is the knowledgeable testimony of Pseudo-George of Arbela, *Exposition of the Offices of the Church*, ed., H.R. Connolly, CSCO 71, 51.

55. Coquin, "Les origines" 146.

56. F.C. Conybeare, *The Key of Truth: A Manual of the Paulician Church of Armenia* (Oxford: Clarendon Press, 1898) lxxviff. I am indebted to Professor Gabriele Winkler for notice of this work.

57. L. Villecourt, "La lettre de Macaire, évêque de Memphis, sur la

liturgie antique du chrême et du baptéme à Alexandrie," *Le Muséon* 36 (1923) 33-46.

58. A. Baumstark, *Nocturna Laus*, Liturgiewissenschaftliche Quellen und Forschungen, vol. 32 (Münster Westfallen, 1957) 30-31 and n. 110.

59. Emmanuel Lanne, "Textes et rites de la liturgie pascale dans l'ancienne Eglise copte," *L'Orient Syrien* 6 (1961) 288f.

60. Villecourt, "Un manuscript arabe" [n. 46 above] 13-19. However, in "La lettre de Macaire" [n. 57 above] he seems to presume both an eight week and a seven week fast.

61. Gérard Viaud, *Les Coptes d'Egypte* (Paris, 1978) 44f.

62. Villecourt, "La lettre de Macaire" 39 and n. 4.

63. Ibid. 34.

64. Ibid. 39. [Emphasis supplied.]

65. B. Evetts, *History of the Patriarchs of the Coptic Church of Alexandria*, PO 1, 5, 10.5 (Paris, 1904-1915), [163] (vol. 1, 427).

66. W.E. Crum, *Der Papyruscodex saec. VI-VII der Phillippsbibliothek in Cheltenham*, Koptische theologische Schriften. Schriften der wissenschaftlichen Gesellschaft in Strassburg, vol. 3 (Strassburg, 1915). I am indebted to P.-M. Gy for his helpful suggestion regarding the determination of the present location of this codex. Unfortunately, neither consultation with H.P. Kraus nor a search of such of the Sotheby sales catalogues as are held by the Pierpont Morgan Library has revealed its whereabouts. The Phillipps catalogue numbered it 18833.

67. Ibid. 67f.

68. Ibid. 69. Columba Stewart, O.S.B. reports (in a personal communication) that in some Tabennesiot monasteries paschal baptism was practiced. This difference from the patriarchal practice, continued in the monasteries of Scete, may throw some light on this account of a rapprochement between the Patriarch and Orsisius.

69. Ibid. 144f.

70. Ibid. 66, n. 4.

71. Evetts, *History of the Patriarchs* [16-22] (vol. 1, 114-120). On the whole matter of the relation of this work to Severus, cf. David W. Johnson, "Further Remarks on the Arabic History of the Patriarchs of Alexandria," *Oriens Christianus*, 61 (Wiesbaden, 1977) 103ff. Johnson tentatively suggests that the author of the earliest materials may have been Mennas the Scribe.

72. Evetts, *History of the Patriarchs* [123] (vol. 1, 387).

73. Ibid. [138, 143] (vol. 1, 402, 407).

74. Ibid. [5] (vol. 1, 402, 407).

75. Cf. note 54 above.

76. Villecourt, "Les observances liturgiques" 314.

77. Ibid. 69. This is still a favored day for baptism in the Coptic rite,

which forbids the ministration of baptism between Palm Sunday and Pentecost [cf. G. Viaud, *Les Coptes d'Egypte* 44].

78. Coquin, "Les origines" 146.

79. Morton Smith, *Clement of Alexandria and a Secret Gospel of Mark* (Cambridge, MA: Harvard University Press, 1973).

80. R.P.C. Hanson, for example, in a generally negative review of Smith's book in the *Journal of Theological Studies*, n.s. 25 (1974), can still say (p. 515): "Patristic scholars can agree that a new letter of Clement of Alexandria has been identified." The fragment is now included in O. Stählin, *Clemens Alexandrinus*, vol. 4, part 1 (2. Aufl., U. Treu, ed.) *Die Griechischen Christlichen Schriftsteller der ersten Jahrhunderte* (Leiden, 1980) xvii-xviii, where current scholarly assessment is very briefly summarized.

81. Smith, *Clement of Alexandria* 446 (folio 1 r°, lines 18-19).

82. Ibid. lines 22-27.

83. Ibid. fol. 1 v°, lines 1-3.

84. Ibid. 447 (fol. 1 v°, line 20 - 2 r°, line 13). [Emphasis supplied.]

85. Cf. Roland Bainton, "The Origins of Epiphany," *Early and Medieval Christianity*, The Collected Papers in Church History, Series One (Boston, 1962) 22-38.

86. Cf. note 7 above, pp. 99-102. On the origin of the prepaschal Lent at Alexandria with Athanasius, cf. Mgr. L. Th. Lefort, "Les lettres festales de saint Athanase," *Bulletin de la Classe des Lettres de l'Académie Royale de Belgique* 39 (1953) 643-656.

87. Villecourt, "Les observances liturgiques."

88. *Ecclesiastical History* V.22.

89. Camillus Callewaert, "La durée et la caractère du Carême ancien dans l'église latine," *Sacris Erudiri* (1940) 651-653, argued that the continuous forty-day period of the fast was counted at Rome beginning with the Sunday of Quadragesima, and came to its conclusion on Thursday of the sixth week, the day on which penitents were reconciled. Such a period would stand just prior to the ancient two-day paschal fast of Friday and Saturday, much as the six-week fast in the East, with its concluding Saturday and Sunday, stood just prior to the extended six-day paschal fast.

90. Cf. Gérard Viaud, *Les Coptes d'Egypte* 78. Louis Villecourt, *Le Muséon* 38 (1925) 269, n. 1 reports the seventeenth-century testimony of J.M. Vansleben that baptism is forbidden between Palm Sunday and Pentecost.

8

The Feasts of All Saints

FROM THE OUTSET, THE PASSION OF THE LORD HAS STOOD AT THE heart of Christian identity. Very quickly, Christians linked witness to the centrality of the cross in human history to participation in that passion. Already at the death of the first martyr, Stephen, the martyr's prayer for his persecutors echoes the prayer of Jesus on the cross for those who knew not what they were about. It was virtually inevitable that, after his conversion to Christ, the one who watched over the outer garments of those who stoned Stephen, consenting to his death, would one day write to the Christians of Rome:

> Do you not know that all of us who have been baptized into Christ Jesus were baptized into his death? We were buried therefore with him by baptism into death, so that as Christ was raised from the dead by the glory of the Father, we too might walk in newness of life. The death he died he died to sin, once for all, but the life he lives he lives to God. So you must consider yourselves dead to sin and alive to God in Christ Jesus.[1]

To profess faith in Christ is already to have entered upon the way of his cross, which for Stephen and Paul and so many others, then and thereafter, came to perfect consummation in martyrdom. To die in witness to Christ was called, "baptism of blood," and martyrdom was sometimes seen as the true baptism of which our baptism in water is but sign and promise.

It is not surprising, therefore, that the early church viewed the ranks of the martyrs as an eschatological embodiment of redemption in Christ. Already in the Apocalypse, the army of the martyrs presents the image of the heavenly church, the fulfillment of the earthly church.

> After this I looked, and behold, a great multitude which no man could number, from every nation, from all tribes and peoples and tongues, standing before the throne and before the Lamb, clothed in white robes, with palm branches in their hands, and crying out with a loud voice, "Salvation belongs to our God who sits upon the throne, and to the Lamb!"
>
> Then one of the elders addressed me, saying, "Who are these, clothed in white robes, and whence have they come?" I said to him, "Sir, you know." And he said to me, "These are they who have come out of the great tribulation; they have washed their robes and made them white in the blood of the Lamb. Therefore are they before the throne of God, and serve him day and night within his temple; and he who sits upon the throne will shelter them with his presence.[2]

Veneration of a Martyr

The early Christians greatly venerated individual martyrs and made their burial places the sites of annual memorials of their passions. This was true even in the second century, as we see in the *Martyrdom of Polycarp*, written from the Church of Smyrna to that of Philomelium, probably in 156.[3] The account relates how the Christians gathered the remains of the martyred bishop from the ashes and deposited them in a place accessible to the community for the purpose of regular memorials:

> There the Lord will permit us, so far as possible, to gather together in joy and gladness to celebrate the day of his martyrdom as a birthday, in memory of those athletes who have gone before, and to train and make ready those who are to come hereafter.[4]

At the outset, indeed, Christians seem to have held no festivals of martyrs apart from those at their tombs, although a bit later the fame of certain prominent martyrs led to their memorials also being held in other cities.[5] It was not always the case, however, that the church was able to recover and bury the remains of the martyrs, as it did for Polycarp. Acts 8:2 tells us that devout men buried Stephen and made lamentation over him, but the location of the tomb did not survive in the memory of the Jerusalem community. We do not know whether an earlier tomb was lost in the destruction of the city in the second century, but several chapels claimed to have his relics prior to their discovery in the fifth century.[6] The protomartyr already had a festival at Jerusalem (and elsewhere when his remains were discovered in 415. In any case, we may be sure that in the fourth century the veneration of the martyrs had grown far beyond local memorials at their tombs.

Veneration of All Martyrs

So violent were the persecutions in the early fourth century that the church's very early appreciation of the company of martyrs as the Church Triumphant began to be expressed in the liturgical calendars of the latter part of the century. One such commemoration of all the martyrs appears in an originally Greek martyrology preserved in a Syriac manuscript written at Edessa in 411/12.[7] This festival was not on a fixed date, but on the Friday in Easter week—the week often devoted to the mystagogical catecheses, which expounded to the neophytes the mysteries into which they had just been initiated. While nothing in this notice of the commemoration of all the martyrs speaks of such catechesis, the occurrence of the festival in this week does bring to mind the much earlier text of the *Martyrdom of Polycarp* and its recognition of the importance of the remembrance of the martyrs for the training of athletes still to come.

We know nothing more of the commemoration of all the martyrs on Easter Friday, but another such commemoration, also on a moveable date, had a wider history. It is the festival of the martyrs on the Sunday following Pentecost, the day marked in western calendars in recent centuries as the feast of the Holy

Trinity. Pentecost, of course, marked the conclusion of the fifty days of paschal celebration, and so was the point at which the community resumed its discipline of fasting. In the later fourth century, however, the integrity of that fifty-day period of rejoicing was beginning to be broken, especially by the celebration of the Ascension of Christ on the fortieth day. This festival appears in a list of feasts in *Apostolic Constitutions* (V.20.2), a canonical and liturgical collection assembled in the neighborhood of Antioch, probably in the last quarter of the fourth century. The same document notes that the community is to resume fasting in the second week after Pentecost (cf. V.20.14). An octave celebration of Pentecost was something not yet seen elsewhere, and so it may be that the resumption of fasting here is only postponed until after the Sunday after Pentecost, a commemoration of all the martyrs. Even so, such a festival as an extension of the paschal rejoicing would be tantamount to an octave of Pentecost.

More explicit mention of such an observance comes from a homily of St. John Chrysostom, a *Laudatio sanctorum omnium qui martyrium toto terrarum orbe sunt passi*. The sermon opens with the announcement that it has been just seven days since the church celebrated the solemnity of the Pentecost.[8] The year in which Chrysostom preached the homily is not known, and therefore we do not know whether he preached it in Antioch or in Constantinople. If at Antioch, where he preached from 386-398, then this memorial of all the martyrs could well have been the day from The morrow of which the Antiochene *Apostolic Constitutions* marked the resumption of normal fasting. If, however, it was preached after St. John Chrysostom became Patriarch of Constantiople in 398, it would mark our earliest testimony there to the feast of All Saints, still observed on the Sunday after Pentecost in the Byzantine rite.[9]

If the celebration of All Saints on the Sunday after Pentecost is now identified especially with the Byzantine rite, this practice was not always exclusively oriental. The earliest epistle list for Rome, the *Comes* of Wurzburg, gives the readings used in the later sixth or very early seventh century, although the list is preserved only in an eighth-century manuscript.[10] There the week following Pentecost is fully articulated with stations: Monday at St. Peter *ad vincula*, Tuesday at St. Anastasia, Wednesday (with two readings from Acts) at St. Mary Major, Thursday at Holy Apostles, Friday at SS. John and Paul, and another reading presumably to be used on Saturday, its station at St. Stephen's. The next appointment is for *Dominica in natale sanctorum*, the epistle appointed being the passage from the Apocalypse quoted above and still assigned to the feast of All Saints on 1 November.

This is a rare testimony to the festival at Rome on the Sunday after Pentecost. This Sunday was formerly the conclusion of the all-night vigil of Ember Saturday, concluding the Embertide that solemnized the resumption of normal fasting after Paschaltide. In the fifth-century preaching of Leo I, the summer Embertide is designated *Ieiunio Pentecostes*, but in the Wurzburg *Comes* the lessons for the Embertide come in the week following the Sunday of All Saints, with the usual Embertide stational assignments: Wednesday at St. Mary Major (with two readings from the Hebrew Bible), Friday at Holy Apostles, and the Saturday vigil at St. Peter's with no Sunday liturgy following. In other words, the resumption of fasting after Paschaltide here follows the pattern noted in the *Apostolic Constitutions*. Here again, then, it appears that All Saints Day is functioning as the octave day of Pentecost.

When, in the eleventh century, Gregory VII definitively restored the summer Embertide to the week following Pentecost, the week retained its character as a festal octave in spite of the fast, and the two lessons of Ember Wednesday remained those from Acts in the Wurzburg *Comes*. The concluding Saturday vigil which once extended to Sunday, leaving it without a proper liturgy, was by then observed earlier in the day on Saturday, and Sunday was the octave day of Pentecost (already observed as the feast of the Holy Trinity in some places).[11] By this time, as we shall see, the feast of All Saints was celebrated on the first day of November.

Dedication of the Pantheon to Christian Use

Rome, however, knew at least one other date for the commemoration of all the martyrs before the adoption of the festival on 1 November. Boniface IV (608-615) obtained permission from the emperor Phocas to convert to Christian use the temple dedicated to all the gods by its builder, Marcus Agrippa, and still today commonly called the Pantheon. This was the first instance at Rome of the conversion of a pagan temple to Christian use, although the practice was common in other parts of the church. The Pantheon was dedicated in 609 to the Blessed Vigin Mary and all the martyrs, evidently on 13 May.[12] Such is the date assigned in the Gregorian Sacramentary to the *Natale Sanctae Mariae ad Martyres*. Giuseppe Löw has observed that in 609, 13 May fell on a Tuesday, while at that time churches were normally dedicated on Sundays. For that reason, he raised the possibility that in choosing that date Boniface IV was influenced by a commemoration of "all the martyrs of the earth" on 13 May, a feast mentioned in the *Carmina Nisibena* by St. Ephrem of Edessa in the fourth century.[13]

The possibility of Edessene influence at Rome, however improbable it may seem, calls attention to a problematic stational assignment in the *Comes* of Wurzburg and the question of its possible relation to the commemoration of all the martyrs in the Syriac martyrology on the Friday after Easter. At the head of the manuscript there is a table of *Capitula*, a sort of table of contents. This puts the station for the liturgy of Easter Sunday *ad sancta maria*, and the table uses the same expression for the station on Friday of Easter week. In the epistle list itself, however, the Sunday station is St. Mary (Major, undoubtedly), while the following Friday's station is *S. Maria Martyra*. Morin, the editor of the manuscript, noted the same expression, *S. Maria Martyra*, on another day in the later list of gospels included in the manuscript. Believing the epistle appointments to come from a date prior to Boniface's dedication of the Pantheon in 609, he suggested that the word *martyra* here was added at the initiative of the eighth-century scribe to reflect the practice of his time. From whatever date, the papal station for Easter Friday is at *S. Maria ad Martyres* in the late eighth-century Sacramentary of Rheinau, in the Gregorian Sacramentary, and, indeed, in *Missale Romanum* right up to Vatican II.

No appointment in these books for that day suggests continuity with the above-mentioned commemoration of all the martyrs on Easter Friday in the Syriac martyrology. However, the Sacramentary of Verona (more commonly called "Leonine"), from which materials for the first three months and part of April are missing, contains in what remains for April a very large number of Mass formularies concerned with unspecified martyrs and saints. Of the known dates for festivals of all the martyrs, none could fall in April save the Friday after Easter in the Syriac martyrology.[14] The Sacramentary of Verona contains no suggestion of a festival of the martyrs on the octave day of Pentecost nor on 13 May. This could suggest that at some point after the dedication of the Pantheon to Mary and the martyrs, the feast honoring all the martyrs was celebrated there on the Friday after Easter, not on the anniversary of the dedication (13 May), although by the time reflected in the Wurzburg *Comes* this festival was observed on the octave day of Pentecost.

Still, while the materials might suffice for the formulation of this or some other hypothesis, they are so complex that it is difficult or impossible to embrace any hypothesis enthusiastically without more study and the willingness to call the established dating of some documents into fresh question. For the present, the tempting data must be left as no more than that.

The commemoration of all the martyrs on the octave day of Pentecost is encountered again in the *Comes* of Murbach. This *Comes* is a schedule of readings intended to accompany the so-called "Gelasian Sacramentaries of the Eighth Century," the family of mixed sacramentaries that preceded Charlemagne's attempt to introduce the Gregorian Sacramentary. There is no further evidence, however, that such a festival took root in Frankish territory. Rather, it was the church of *S. Maria ad martyres*, its *natale* on May 13, which seems to have loomed largest as a focus for the devotion of pilgrims to the memory of the martyrs. Perhaps for this reason, Gregory III (731-741) thoroughly restored and further embellished this church in the eighth century.

From All Martyrs to All Saints

Another initiative of Gregory III, however, significantly broadened the content of the still emerging feast of All Saints. *Liber Pontificalis* (I.417) records that he built a new chapel within the nave of St. Peter's. Marked "38" in Alfarano's plan of the old basilica, it was on the left as one faced the *confessio*, just before the intersection of the transept. Prior to the dedication of this chapel, devotion to the company of the triumphant had focused almost entirely on the martyrs. Here, the dedication is to "the Redeemer, his holy Mother, all the apostles, martyrs, confessors, and all the just and perfect who are at rest throughout the whole world." Gregory appointed a cadre of monks to recite daily vigils in the chapel and a company of priests to celebrate weekly Masses in honor of the saints. Duchesne puts this dedication within the first eight months of 732,[15] but further precision is impossible. His understanding, however, would preclude 1 November.

It is embarrassing that we know so little of the origin of the date for the feast of All Saints, the festival which embodies the content associated with Gregory III's chapel. Bede refers to it in two martyrologies,[16] but his account has been subject to later addition, at least. In 798, Arno, Archbishop of Salzburg, prescribed the festival on 1 November as a precept for all of Southeast Germany at the Synod of Riesbach. The lectionary of Alcuin from about the same period has the festival with a vigil, but his student, Amalarius, makes no mention of it.

It is on writers from the twelfth century that we must depend for our understanding of the final determination of the familiar date for the festival. According to Beleth,[17] the provisions of food available in Rome in the spring were insufficient for both the inhabitants and the hordes of pilgrims who descended upon the city for the festival on 13 May, which moved Gregory IV (827-844) to shift the festival to a point after the harvest, to the date already known in Germany and France, 1 November. Sigebert of Gembloux[18] repeats the earlier notice of the Martyology of Ado[19] that Gregory IV sought and received the support of Louis the Pious for this change of date, adding that it was in 835 that Louis, supported by the bishops of France and Germany, ordered the festival observed throughout the empire. Sigebert, however, continued to ascribe the origin of the festival to Boniface and his rededication of the Pantheon.

Since Alcuin's lectionary, a document prior to the accession of Gregory IV, reports the feast on 1 November complete with a vigil, we must finally leave the question of the origin of the date unresolved. Faced with the ambiguity, however, we probably should consider seriously the possibility that the veneration of all the just and perfect on this day was a Christian response to the

Druid festival of the dead, Samhain, observed on the same date.[20] As our continuing folk celebration of All Hallows Eve reveals, the Druid piety, replete with fairies, witches, and goblins reputed to destroy crops and steal children, proved highly resistant to Christian reinterpretation.

Some have suggested that the institution of all Souls' Day by Odilo of Cluny in 998, beginning with vespers of the dead following second vespers of the feast, was a further Christian response to the "old religion." Whatever continuity this observance has with classical Christian piety, in some cultures it eventually left the commemoration of all the saints framed by the almost equally bizarre phenomena of Halloween and the singing of *Dies Irae* over a black-draped empty coffin.

Sixtus IV, seeking the protection of the saints after the Turkish capture of Otranto in 1480, extended to all the church the obligation of the celebration of All Saints through an octave, a custom that many local churches already followed. Although the octave is no longer observed, the American *Book of Common Prayer* reckons the feast of All Saints among the seven "Principal Feasts" of the church which take precedence over any other observance. The *Book of Common Prayer* also allows the feast to be observed on the Sunday following 1 November in addition to its celebration on that day. Further, together with Easter, Pentecost, and the feast of the Lord's Baptism, the feast of All Saints is a baptismal day. All Saints is a day recommended for the celebration of Christian initiation, for it is into the company of those who have washed their robes and made them white in the blood of the Lamb that we are baptized, dead to sin and alive to God in Christ Jesus. Whatever its consummation, it is there at the font that our life of witness, *martyria*, takes its beginning in our participation in the mystery of Christ's death and resurrection.

Notes

1. Romans 6:3-4, 10-11.
2. Revelation 7:9-10, 13-15.
3. A convenient text is in Cyril Richardson, ed., *Early Christian Fathers* (New York: Macmillan, 1970) 149-158.
4. *Mart. Polycarpi* 18.3, as found in Richardson, *Early Christian Fathers* 156.

5. The Chronograph of 354 announces the burial dates of Roman martyrs, and the cemeteries in which they are buried. Included, however, is Cyprian, his memorial assigned to the cemetery of Callistus. The notice reads: "Of Cyprian of Africa; at Rome he is celebrated [at the cemetery] of Callistus."

6. A. Renoux, *Le Codex Arménien Jérusalem 121*, vol. 1, PO 35.1, no. 35.1, no. 163 (Turnhout, 1969) 36-40; Ibid., vol. 2, PO 36.2, no. 168 (Turnhout, 1971) 369 [231] f.

7. Br. Mus. add. 12050. The most recent edition is that in Latin of Bonaventura Mariani, *Breviarium Syriacum*, Rerum Ecclesiasticarum Documenta, Series Minor. Subsidia Studiorum, vol. 3 (Rome: Herder, 1956). This document lists the martyrs observed in various cities on fixed dates. This commemoration, whose date would vary with the date of Pascha, is reported under 6 April, the date traditionally associated with Pascha in Asia Minor and Syria. Hans Achelis took this to be to precise date for the Friday after Pascha and so supposed that the original list in Greek was prepared in a year in which Easter fell on 1 April.

8. PG 50:705.

9. On this cf. John Baldovin, S.J., "Saints in the Byzantine Tradition," *Liturgy* 5:2 (Fall 1985) 71-75.

10. G. Morin, "Le plus ancien *comes* de l'église romaine," *Revue Bénédictine* 27 (1910) 41-74. In his discussion of the list (pp. 72-74) Morin details the known seventh-century developments in the Roman liturgy not yet represented by this text.

11. Peter Browe, "Zur Geschichte des Dreifältigkeitsfestes," *Archiv für Liturgiewissenschaft* 1 (1950), p. 69 notes the presence of Trinity Sunday on the first Sunday after Pentecost in a sacramentary written at Fulda before 1000.

12. L. Duchesne, *Liber Pontificalis*, vol. 1, 317, n. 2: "La dédicace du Panthéon est marquée au 13 mai dans le petit martyrologe romain et dans celui d'Adon, d'où cette indication a passé aux martyrologes posterieurs." Bede, *Hist. Ang.* 2.4, gives an account of the conversion of the Pantheon similar to that in the *Liber Pontificalis*, in the context of his description of the *ad limina* of Mellitus, Bishop of London, and his participation in a synod in Rome in 610. Bede says: "After solemn purification, Boniface consecrated it as the Church of the Holy Mother of God and all Christian Martyrs; and once its horde of devils had been cast out, it became a memorial to the Company of Saints." However, he, too, fails to give a precise date for the consecration.

13. Guiseppe Löw, "Ognissanti," *Enciclopedia Cattolica*, vol. 9, col. 87.

14. C.L. Feltoe, *Sacramentarium Leonianum* (Cambridge, 1896), p. 173, sought to relate these formularies to the consecration of the Pantheon in the following month. C. Mohlberg, *Sacramentarium Veronense* (Rome:

Herder, 1956), p. lxxxi, calls attention to the opinion of Scipione Maffei that certain of these were for a feast of All Saints (with octave) established by Boniface IV.

15. *Liber Pontificalis*, vol. 1, 423.

16. PL 94:606; 94:1087.

17. *Rationale* 127 (PL 202:133f.).

18. *Chronicon*, ad anno 835 (PL 160:159).

19. *Martyrologia*, Kal. Nov. (PL 123:387).

20. James H. Barnett, "Halloween," *Encyclopedia Britannica*, vol. 11 (1960), 106f.

9

The Liturgical Year:
Pattern of Proclamation

PRECEDING CHAPTERS HAVE EXAMINED PARTICULAR FEASTS AND SEA-
sons, but the liturgical year is more than a string of discrete
observances. The concern of this chapter will be to look at the seasonal cycle as a whole. Although this will require further examination of still other particular festivals, we need to see the tem-
poral cycle as a frame for the ordered proclamation of the Gospel.

The Liturgical Year in Protestantism

The ordering of scripture reading within a pattern of festivals
and seasons called "the liturgical year" has long been characteristic of churches that are described as "liturgical," especially the
Roman Catholic, Orthodox, Lutheran, and Anglican Churches.
Over these past decades, however, such a liturgical articulation of
time has become characteristic of most of the Christian churches
in North America, a development since Vatican II that is so
broadly ecumenical that we can hardly find one main line de-
nomination that is not concerned with questions of lectionary
and the liturgical year.

One must confess immediately, however, that such a claim for
consensus can be overstated. Some scholars of a strongly reformed tradition are making their own contributions to studies in
liturgical time, even though these often take the negative view
that such ordered worship life represents a decay of New Testament spirituality.

125

As a case in point, Karel Deddens, a Reformed scholar in Holland, published in 1975 a dissertation that assigned the development of the liturgical year to Cyril of Jerusalem in the middle of the fourth century.[1] On this basis, he argues that the notion of a liturgical cycle of feasts and seasons is characteristic of Christianity's altered situation following its accommodation to the Roman Empire during the reign of Constantine. As such, the liturgical year represents a deviation from the purity of the spirituality of the early church, and must be regarded as a symptom of that ritualism from which the Reformation, and especially Calvin, liberated Christianity. The notion of a liturgical year, Deddens concludes, is inconsistent with New Testament spirituality.

This is not a surprising conclusion for a Dutch Calvinist to reach. What is challenging is that he does this on the basis of an analysis of the role of Cyril of Jerusalem that he found in *The Shape of the Liturgy* by the important Anglican Benedictine liturgist, Gregory Dix. Dix was not alone in assigning the liturgical year to such a late date; a fourth-century origin for the liturgical year has been virtually a commonplace among scholars in the field, though not least through the influence of Dom Gregory.

Dix not only assigned a key role to Cyril in the shaping of the liturgical year; he also urged that the church in the fourth century had put aside her primitive eschatological outlook in favor of a "new historical interest" that set Christ's saving work in the past rather than in the present experience of the worshiping community. More recent studies, however, argue that this is a curious and insupportable dichotomy.[2] Consciousness of our historical past and especially of the historical rootedness of the salvific work of Christ is not an alternative to eschatological expectation, but is the ground of this expectation. Memory engenders hope. Such a principle is deeply ingrained in all Judeo-Christian tradition.

The liturgical year, I want to argue, is not an invention of the fourth century, but is a Christian development from roots that are continuous with the Old Testament. However, the phrase, "liturgical year," does deserve a word of explanation. It has not always been a common expression in liturgical law, and should not be supposed to have been, in precisely that phrase, a common concern in the tradition. The liturgical year (as we shall continue to call it) does not refer and has never referred to a systematic liturgical articulation of every day or even every week in the year. Rather, it refers to an appreciation of annual (as opposed to weekly) occasions of celebration, such as would observe one or more annual festivals that would stand apart from the regular weekly observance of Sabbath (for Jews) or Sunday (for Christians). Our present view of the origins of the Christian liturgical year puts that development much earlier than Dix supposed. In what follows, I am dependent on many important scholars, but much is yet hypothesis for which the argument is detailed in my longer study of *The Origins of the Liturgical Year*.[3] With that admission, I shall, in the interest of clarity, omit the complex arguments and qualifications provided there, and simply report my conclusions.

Liturgical Week and Liturgical Year

We have long been accustomed to say that the primitive church observed no annual festivals, but only the first day of each week as celebration of the Lord's resurrection. Even in the light of more recent studies, this seems to have been true for the Gentile churches, those not of the circumcision that were not expected to observe the prescriptions of the Law regarding festivals. This would not apply to Jewish Christians, however. The primitive community at Jerusalem did not stop praying in the temple, nor can we suppose that they ceased to celebrate Passover. Indeed, they would have found the Preparation of the Passover, the day of the sacrifice of the lambs for the festival, charged with a new meaning as the anniversary of the death of the Lord, who, according to the Fourth Gospel, died on the cross at the hour of the offering of the lambs. This primitive fixing of the date of the passion seems to be presumed already in St. Paul's proclamation to the Corinthians (ca. A.D. 55) that "Christ our paschal lamb has been sacrificed" (1 Cor 5:7). There is no reason to doubt that this new content of Passover was at least informally present to the Jerusalem community's keeping of this festival already in the year following the resurrection. Even if they, and the other churches, had already begun to gather on the first day of the week, it would be only to this extent that we could say that the

Christian week is older than the Christian year. Surely, by the end of the first century the observance of Sunday was universal; the Christian observance of Passover, however, was not. Nonetheless, our annual paschal celebration is not a new Christian invention, but is in direct continuity with the Passover traditions of the Old Testament, albeit now with a new focus on the saving work of Jesus, the Christ, the paschal lamb of a covenant renewed.

This tradition, however, underwent further reshaping in the second century. The majority of the Jerusalem community was dispersed following Hadrian's destruction of the city and his building of a new Roman city on the rubble of Jerusalem in the early 130s. To insure that there would be no resumption of troubles with the Jews, all the circumcised were forbidden to enter the new city, Aelia Capitolina, and this rule excluded Jewish Christians as well. These were dispersed, continuing a diaspora that may have begun already during the troubles leading to the destruction of the Temple in A.D. 70. A major center for this Christian resettlement was Asia Minor, and it is there especially that we find our richest evidence for a continuing Christian observance of Passover and the following Pentecost in the second century. These Christians, however, had been separated from the synagogues since the final decade of the first century, and so were put in an awkward position regarding the celebration of the annual Passover. The date of the festival was set by scripture in the night from the 14th to the 15th of Nisan, the first spring month; but the Jewish lunar calendar, being some eleven days shorter than a solar year, had a month added from time to time as needed, in order to keep pace with the seasons. The decision as to when to add an extra month was made by the rabbis in Palestine, and the Christians of Asia could not continue to depend on their authority, nor is it clear how Christians could learn of their decisions. Therefore, the Asian Christians simply adopted the local solar calendar, and observed the paschal fast on the fourteenth day of the first month of spring, a sufficiently close parallel to the Jewish date, and not the only variant method of determining the critical fourteenth day of the first month.[4] The months in this Asian form of the Julian calendar began nine days earlier than the months at Rome,[5] and when the Roman calendar was adopted with the founding of Constantinople in 330, this Asian fixed date for the Preparation of the Passover, the fourteenth day of a month called Artemisios, was expressed as 6 April. Failure to recognize this date, 6 April, as the Roman calendar's equivalent to the fourteenth day of the first spring month in the calendar used in Asia Minor in the second century has been a major stumbling block to understanding the early development of our festivals.[6] We shall return to this paschal date, still observed as Passover by Montanists in the fifth century, according to a historian of that time.[7]

With the departure of the bishops of the circumcision from Jerusalem, a Gentile episcopate was established, and the first such bishop, from around 135, was Marcus. Evidently, this brought into close conjunction (and perhaps conflict) the Gentile custom of observing only the first day of the week and the Jewish Christian observance of the annual Passover. The resulting compromise called for keeping Passover, but with the termination of the paschal fast only on the day of the resurrection, Sunday. This custom was adopted quickly at Alexandria, and spread rapidly through the Gentile churches, although it seems to have been adopted at Rome only around A.D. 165, the first year of the episcopate of Soter.[8] However, as in several other places, a small Asian community in Rome seems to have continued to observe the fixed Passover date, unadjusted to the day of the week. They came to be called "Fourteenthers" or Quartodecimans, and were a continuing thorn in the side of the Roman bishops attempting to hold in unity that many-faceted cosmopolitan community. The continuing ties of the Asians in Rome to their bishop in Ephesus, and his support of their paschal date, led eventually to the struggle in the late second century, which ended in the excommunication of the province of Asia by Victor, Bishop of Rome.[9] This outrageous act had little effect, in fact, and the determination of the date of Easter was, after Arianism, the second major item on the agenda of the Council of Nicea in 325. Only then appeared a general agreement that Easter should be on Sunday, although this was surely the predominant practice throughout the third century.

The Asian observance orignally entailed a fast commemorating the passion and death of the Lord on the day of Preparation of the

Passover, and a vigil through the night, concluded with eucharist at cockcrow. When this was adjusted to the structure of the week, the vigil was through the night from Saturday to Sunday, and the concluding eucharist came at cockcrow on Sunday. The one-day fast now fell on Saturday, although such made this one Saturday in the year an exception to the general Jewish and Eastern Church tradition forbidding fasting on the Sabbath.[10] This one day was now adjacent to the weekly fast on Friday, established already in the first century.[11] We learn from Irenaeus in the second century that some fasted for one day, but others connected the Friday and Saturday and fasted for two days.[12] By the middle of the third century, it is clear that in some places the first four days of the week had been added as less rigorous fast days, giving us the Holy Week we now know. The earliest source for this extension of the paschal fast to six days, the *Didascalia Apostolorum*, reveals a curious chronology evidently derived from the calendar of the Essenes at Qumran, a calendar so wedded to the seven day week that its year consisted of exactly fifty-two weeks and, therefore, only 364 days. This put every month date on the same day of the week in every year, and Passover, begun at sundown of the 14th day of the first month, was always celebrated in the night from Tuesday to Wednesday.[13] The *Didascalia Apostolorum* says that we fast on Monday because on this day Judas made his treasonous compact with the priests; we fast on Tuesday because then the Lord ate the Passover with his disciples; on Wednesday he was arrested; on Thursday he was brought before Pilate. On all these four days the fast may be broken at the ninth hour (mid-afternoon). On Friday and Saturday one fasted entirely, however, in commemoration of the death of Christ and his lying in the tomb.[14]For reasons that are less than clear, commentators have often denied that we see any trace of Good Friday before the fourth century, and Dix, we have seen, assigned the invention of Holy Week to Cyril, Bishop of Jerusalem, in the latter half of that century.[15] In fact, our observance of Holy Week is in full view a century before Cyril, including a solemn fast on the Friday in commemoration of the Lord's death.

In both the Asian fixed date Pascha and in its adjustment to the structure of the week, the Sunday Pascha, the character of the celebration was the same: a commemoration of the entire mystery of our redemption by Christ on the occasion of his passion.[16] This included the passion, death, resurrection, and glorification of the Lord, and the outpouring of the Spirit upon the church. Indeed, the incarnation itself was included among the themes celebrated. This led eventually to the assignment of the conception of Christ to the date associated with the passion, 6 April. St. Ephrem of Edessa, in one of his paschal hymns, wrote:

> In Nisan the Lord of Thunder weakened his heart through sympathy and entered into the womb of Mary that he might dwell there; in Nisan again he has shown himself strong, and after loosing the womb of hell is risen.[17]

At this point, however, we must admit a further complication. As we said earlier, 6 April is the Roman calendar date equivalent to the fourteenth of the first spring month, Artemisios, in the pre-Constantinian calendar of Asia Minor. At Rome itself, by the early third century, historical interest, perhaps prompted by commemoration of the martyrs on the days of their deaths, led to an attempt to establish the exact Julian calendar date for the crucifixion. This would not be a translation of the 14th of Nisan into the first month of a solar calendar as was the Asian date, but rather the determination of the Roman calendar date on which the 14th day of Nisan fell in the year of our Lord's passion. In other words, the Roman question did not concern itself with how to convert the Passover date from a lunar to a solar calendar, but with the precise Julian date on which our Lord died. The year was determined, rightly or wrongly, to be A.D. 29, and in that year the 14th of Nisan, the 14th day of the spring moon, was computed to have fallen on 25 March. This, therefore, was taken in the West to be the date of the crucifixion. In time, 25 March, too, was taken to be the date of both the death and the conception of the Lord. We have texts from Augustine and others that explicitly identify the dates of the conception and passion of the Lord and base the nativity date of 25 December on the conception/passion date of 25 March, the nativity being just nine months after the conception.[18]

Computation of the Nativity Date

For two centuries it has been popular to say that Christmas is a Christian adoption and adaptation of the Roman pagan festival *Dies natalis solis invicti*, the birthday of the invincible Sun. That was not a festival of great antiquity at Rome. It was established on 25 December, the traditional (but inaccurate) winter solstice date, by the Emperor Aurelian in the Year of our Lord 274. Those who seek to base Christmas on this festival seldom give full weight to its late institution. In fact, in support of this theory of a pagan Sun festival as origin for our nativity feast, many writers point to the mosaic ceiling in the mausoleum of the Julii in the Vatican cemetery, a mosaic showing Christ as the Sun, driving his chariot across the heavens.[19] In fact, archaeologists assign the mosaic to a time some decades before there was a pagan festival on 25 December, although Christ was already associated with the sun on the basis of Malachi 4:2. Nor, it now seems, should we appeal to Constantine's syncretism for the adoption of such a pagan festival (*pace* Cullmann[20]). It seems highly likely that Christmas was being observed in North Africa before the accession of Constantine.[21] On the other hand, from at least 324 forward, Constantine had little contact with the city of Rome, being preoccupied with his new Christian capital of Constantinople, and there is no sign of a feast of Christ's nativity on 25 December at Constantinople during Constantine's lifetime.[22]

At Rome, Leo's Christmas sermons in the fifth century reveal his awareness of the coincidence of the nativity feast with the sun festival of the old religion, and he warns against confusing the two; but we cannot escape the texts from the fourth and following centuries that reveal the thinking of Christians of that time on the question of the origin of the date of Christmas. It was on 25 December because this was nine months from the historical date of his passion, and he was conceived on the day on which he died, 25 March. The earliest known evidence of a claim that the western Christmas was based on a pagan festival appears in the final decades of the twelfth century.[23] In view of the texts already cited and others from the sixth and seventh centuries that reveal in East and West the computation of the nativity date from that assigned to the death and conception,[24] it would seem that those who want to argue for a pagan origin for the nativity festival must present some firm evidence. Failing this, we are left with contemporary voices who say that it was this assignment of the annunciation to the date of the passion that yielded the nativity date nine months later, in the East on 6 January, and later in the West on 25 December.

While there is every reason to believe that such a computation to 6 January was first made in Asia Minor, by whose calendar the April paschal date was established, nonetheless, by the end of the second century this date was known to Clement of Alexandria. He observes in his *Stromateis* (I.21.145) that Christ was born 194 years and one month and thirteen days before the death of the Emperor Commodus (on 31 December 192). Several writers in the past computed this birth date by the Julian calendar and concluded that Clement of Alexandria thought that Jesus was born on 18 November. However, Roland Bainton, in the course of his doctoral research at Yale,[25] showed that at this point Clement was dependent on a source from the Egyptian countryside that still followed the old Egyptian calendar, which did not have a leap-year. Those who figured the birth of Jesus on 18 November, therefore, counted forty-nine days too many (the number of leap-years in this period of 194 years). When these forty-nine days are restored, it becomes clear that the date to which Clement referred was, in fact, 6 January.[26] The immediately following section of Clement's *Stromateis* is the comparatively well known passage in which Clement observes that the Basilidians "also" celebrate the baptism of Jesus on this date, and Bainton established a similar practice for the Marcionites.

Given the observance of the same date by groups separated from one another, it now seems that we must suppose the Epiphany to have been established at some point rather early in the second century, first, I suspect, in Asia Minor, and spreading from there to Syria, Palestine, and Egypt.

It was once thought that the Epiphany must have been based on some pagan festival, perhaps first in Egypt. Indeed, the distinguished German philologist, Eduard Norden, argued that 6 January was the date of a winter solstice festival in Egypt in 1996 B.C., but that by the time of the founding of Alexandria in the fourth century B.C., due to a calendar error of one day every 128 years, the solstice actually fell on 25 December.[27] While this argument has found a prominent place in subsequent literature,[28] the calendar error to which Norden referred is that in the Julian calendar, a system devised only in 45 B.C. and therefore nonexistent in the twentieth century B.C. It is only from the standpoint of that calendar that we can speak of the winter solstice falling on a Julian date in the twentieth century before Christ. Astronomers find it useful to do so, and it was from such an astronomical table for the vernal equinox that Norden took his data. His assertion was astronomically precise, but historically meaningless. The ancient Egyptian calendar had just 365 days per year, as noted above. Its error was not one day every 128 years, but one day every *four* years, and this in the opposite direction from the error of which Norden spoke. Norden's attempt to account for the Epiphany date of 6 January is fatally flawed, and must be retired.

Beyond this attempt to account for the date, testimonies that have been invoked on behalf of a pagan festival on 6 January fail to stand up to close examination,[29] and now it can be fairly said that we have no evidence of a significant pagan festival on 6 January; nor is it possible to imagine any such syncretism in second-century Christianity. Failing this, we must again take it that the date was established by counting nine months from the date associated with the primitive paschal celebration of the entire mystery of Christ, the passion, resurrection and glorification, but also the incarnation.

The Year and the Proclamation of the Gospel

An Egyptian source of the fourth century refers to the Epiphany as the celebration of the Baptism of Jesus, and says that this feast is the beginning of the year.[30] What does this mean? What begins on the Epiphany? We have suggested that the date was computed as that of Christ's nativity, the beginning of his earthly life. Clement seems to have known this, but he also knows of the celebration of Christ's baptism on this date, the beginning of Jesus' public ministry and the occasion of the anointing with the Spirit by virtue of which Jesus is revealed as Messiah.

Years ago, Allan McArthur suggested that in second century Ephesus the Epiphany marked the beginning of the course reading of the Gospel of John, a reading brought to its conclusion with the reading of this gospel's passion narrative at Pascha.[31] In my own study of the origins of the Christian year I have suggested that the same was or became true of the Gospel of Matthew at Jerusalem and of the Gospel of Mark at Alexandria. The complex themeology of the Epiphany derives from the variety in the beginnings of the Gospels, one or another of which, I believe, was read on the Epiphany. Matthew begins with the nativity story, including the visit of the Magi; Mark with the baptism of Jesus in the Jordan; John with both of these, perhaps, but in close connection with the wedding at Cana.

The supposition of such a course reading of Mark at Alexandria is especially compelling, and allows us to appreciate more fully our own lenten liturgy. It also offers an explanation of the curiosity that on Palm Sunday, over the three years of the lectionary, we read the accounts of the entry into Jerusalem and then the passion according to one or another of the synoptic Gospels, although none of them suggests any chronological connection between the two events. Such a reconstruction, however, shows us an extremely complex development in which the forty-day fast originated not as preparation for Easter, but following immediately after the Epiphany, while still a time of preparation for baptism at the conclusion of these forty days.[32]

A generation ago, liturgical historians loved to deride the association of Lent with the fast of Jesus as a late symbolic reinterpretation of a season of fasting that had its beginning in the preparation of candidates for baptism at Easter. More recently, we have become a bit more cautious in urging the universality of paschal baptism in the first centuries of our era. In Egypt, especially, baptism was not at first conferred at Easter, nor is it today. In current Coptic practice, baptisms are forbidden between Palm Sunday and Pentecost, and this seems to reflect a very primitive tradition in Egypt, where Epiphany began the reading of the Gospel of Mark with the celebration of the baptism of Jesus in Jordan. On the next day, following the chronology laid down in the Gospel, Jesus began his fast in the wilderness, and so the church began its observance of the forty-day fast. This was in imitation of the fast of Jesus, but it also provided an opportunity for the final shaping of candidates for baptism. In the sixth and final week of the fast, baptism was conferred, and on a day that Coptic tradition associated with the conferral of baptism by Jesus. The source of this curious tradition regarding Jesus baptizing on the day on which the Alexandrian Church baptized was a puzzle that long defied solution, but for the past decade I have been obsessed with the idea that we now have the source of that tradition in the so-called secret gospel of Mark, quoted in a letter of Clement of Alexandria discovered by Prof. Morton Smith and first published in 1973, a gospel passage read, Clement says, only to those being initiated into the great mysteries. This added passage in Alexandria's version of Mark closely parallels John's story of the raising of Lazarus, but includes an account of Jesus' subsequent initiation of the young man he had raised from the dead. The text and the contextual documents have been examined above in chapter 7.

The secret gospel occurs in chapter 10 of Mark, following verse 34 of the canonical text, and our Coptic sources tell us that the season of fast was brought to a celebratory conclusion on the Sunday following the baptisms with the Feast of Palms, the celebration of Christ's entry into Jerusalem at the beginning of the following chapter 11 of Mark. It was this Feast of Palms, Coptic writers tell us, that was the conclusion of the fast of forty days, not the Pascha of the resurrection that was kept in its own time in the month of Nisan. Between Mark's account of the entry into Jerusalem and the passion narrative there are a few chapters devoted to the teachings of Jesus, but without any narrative story line.[33] These, we may believe, were read as needed during the neutral zone (we would call it the "green season") between Palm Sunday and the paschal fast of six days or less during which the passion narrative was read. Thus, it appears, the liturgical year from Epiphany to Easter was shaped by the course reading of the Gospel of Mark in the Church of Alexandria from as early as the second century.

The Forty-Day Fast before Pascha

Late but uncontradicted sources observe that the Nicene settlement of the date of Easter included the decision to put the major fast before Pascha, as was already customary where baptism was performed at Easter, and to set its length at forty days, retaining Egypt's custom of imitating the fast of Jesus. The Eastern Churches understood this to mean setting the fast of forty days prior to the paschal fast of six days, yielding a six-week Lent followed by Holy Week. At Constantinople, the ancient Egyptian course reading of Mark during the imitative fast was adopted. On the fifth Sunday of Lent all the Byzantine rite churches still read Mark 10:32-45, the old Coptic chapter 31 into which the story of the miracle at Bethany was inserted. By the time of our earliest evidence for Constantinople, a sermon of John Chrysostom, the canonical text of Mark has evidently rejected the secret gospel that had been read at the conferral of baptism, and the Saturday of Lazarus after that fifth Sunday drops Mark abruptly in favor of John, to read the only canonical parallel to the secret gospel, the story of the raising of Lazarus, on a day that still bears the marks of a major baptismal liturgy, even though but a week before the Paschal Vigil. The Saturday of Lazarus is followed by Palm Sunday, its account of the entry into Jerusalem also read from John, the only Gospel in which the entry is chronologically related to the passion. During the paschal fast itself, Holy Week, the Byzantine gospels are drawn from Matthew, readings obviously taken over from Jerusalem. After Nicea, therefore, it would seem that Constantinople adopted the old Alexandrian course reading of Mark for Lent, but broke its relation to Epiphany and set it prior to Holy Week. The ending of this course with the rejected secret gospel was impossible, and John's account of the Bethany miracle was substituted, as was John's account of the entry into Jerusalem on the following day. Thus it came to pass that Palm Sunday, having originated six weeks after Epiphany, was kept after Nicea on the Sunday at the head of the paschal fast of six days.

Pilgrims from Constantinople to Jerusalem insisted on visiting the places they heard of in the gospels on the days on which they heard of them, and we find the pilgrim Egeria in 383 recounting that already established were a liturgical visit to the tomb of Lazarus at Bethany on the day before Palm Sunday, and a procession with palms down the Mount of Olives on the Sunday at the head of the paschal fast. The procession with palms seems to be native to Jerusalem, although the reason for it on this day, as with the visit to the tomb of Lazarus on the previous day, was evidently an influence from Constantinople. This impressive procession rite was carried from Jerusalem to Spain and elsewhere in Europe by returning pilgrims, and eventually it was adopted at Rome as well, although by this time Rome dedicated this Sunday to the reading of the Passion of Matthew. So the double theme of the Sunday is still found in the liturgy of our own day. That we read the synoptic Gospels for both the entry and the passion, gospels that establish no chronological connection between the two events, heightens the importance of the processional hymnody that supplies that dimension of the Johannine chronology in such lines as, "to thee before thy passion they sang their hymns of praise," and "ride on, ride on in majesty; in lowly pomp ride on to die."

If the Gospels take us no further than the resurrection, we still have evidence from the second century of the observance of the Great Fifty Days of rejoicing with the prohibition of fasting and kneeling in prayer. That discipline of unbroken rejoicing was reiterated at the Council of Nicea, but this seems to have been an action taken in response to perceived decay in the integrity of the pentecost. At Jerusalem to the end of the fourth century the final day of this joyous period marked both the ascension of Jesus and the gift of the Spirit, but elsewhere the ascension began to be observed on the fortieth day. In Brescia this festival was itself preceded by a fast that, in fifth-century Gaul, was supplied with litanical processions on the three days before the ascension, namely, the Rogation Days that achieved such popularity in medieval Europe. Overcoming this decay of the integrity of the Paschal Pentecost has, as we know, been one major emphasis of recent reforms of the liturgical year. Such insistence on the unity of the glorification of Christ with the Spirit's indwelling of the church has perhaps had no finer statement than that of Leo the Great in the fifth century. In one of his sermons on the Ascension he said, "all that was visible of the Redeemer has passed over into the sacraments"; and we must recall that for Leo "sacraments" included festivals and the entire liturgical complex.

In these holy mysteries Christ lives, consecrating all the ages that remain until that final parousia for which we watch in hope.

It is to enliven this hope that we recall the story of our redemption, for only memory can open the future to hope, and the form taken by recalling the Gospel of our redemption is the liturgical year.

The liturgical year as we encounter it today represents the weaving together of many local traditions, but this complex development is only the result of ecumenical convergence upon a primitive simple insistence on the historicity of our salvation, an insistence that prompted the writing of the Gospels and their proclamation in the liturgical assemblies for which they were written. All the seasonal phenomena of our worship—Advent wreaths, the Christmas crèche, Epiphany water, ashes, palms, the paschal candle—all have grown not out of the imitation of pagan surroundings, but out of the imaginative and affective response of the people of God in generation after generation to the proclamation of this one story of one life and one death that became the story of their lives as it is the story of ours. This life and saving death and resurrection are celebrated at every eucharist, but the telling of the story, the proclamation of its history, is the origin and the present purpose of the liturgical year, a pattern of proclamation that is not only consistent with New Testament spirituality, but native to it.

Notes

1. Karel Deddens, *Annus Liturgicus? Een onderzoek naar de betekenis van Cyrillus van Jerusalem voor de ontwikkeling van het 'kerkelijk jaar'* (Goes: Oosterbaan & Le Cointre, 1975).

2. Cf. especially Robert Taft, S.J., "Historicism Revisited," *Beyond East and West: Problems in Liturgical Understanding*, NPM Studies in Church Music and Liturgy (Washington, D.C.: The Pastoral Press, 1984) 15-30.

3. T.J. Talley, *The Origins of the Liturgical Year* (New York: Pueblo Publishing Co., 1986).

4. Polycrates of Ephesus, writing late in the second century, is convinced that he, like his forebears, continues to observe "the day when the people put away the leaven" [Eusebius, *Ecclesiastical History* V.24.6]. Whether this means that the Church of Ephesus still followed the lunar calendar is unclear.

5. On this Asian recension of the Julian calendar, cf. Th. Mommsen,

"Die Einführung des asianischen kalendars," *Gesammelte Schriften*, vol. 5 (Berlin: Weidermann, 1908) 518-528.

6. Roland Bainton, e.g., in an important essay cited in note 25 below, insisted that 6 April was not a significant solar date and therefore supposed that references to it represented a computation backward from 6 January, itself taken over from a pagan festival.

7. Sozomen, *Ecclesiastical History* VII.18.

8. Cf. chapter 6 above and also Marcel Richard, "La Question pascale au IIᵉ siècle," *L'Orient Syrien* 6 (1961) 179-212; Karl Holl, "Ein Bruchstück aus einem bisher unbekannten Brief des Epiphanus," *Gesammelte Aufsätze zur Kirchengeschichte*, vol. 2 (Tübingen: Mohr, 1928) 204-224.

9. Cf. George La Piana, "The Roman Church at the End of the Second Century," *Harvard Theological Review* 18 (1925) 201-277.

10. This prohibition against fasting on the Sabbath was also in effect in Africa, at least among the Montanists. Cf. Tertullian, *De ieiuniis* 14.

11. *Didache* 8.

12. Eusebius, *Ecclesiastical History* V.24.12.

13. On this calendar, cf. Annie Jaubert, *The Date of the Last Supper* (Staten Island, NY: Alba House, 1965).

14. R.H. Connolly, *Didascalia Apostolorum* (Oxford: Clarendon Press, 1929) 181f.

15. Gregory Dix, *The Shape of the Liturgy* (London: Dacre, 1945) 350ff.

16. Cf. Odo Casel, "Art und Sinn der ältesten christlichen Osterfeier," *Jahrbuch für Liturgiewissenschaft* 14 (1938) 1ff.

17. *Hymnus XXI de resurrectione Christi*, verse 10, as found in Th. J. Lamy, *Ephraemi Syri hymni et sermones*, vol. 2 (Mechliniae, 1886) 774.

18. *De Trinitate* IV.5; *Quaestionum in Heptateuchum* II.90. Cf. also the tractate *De soltitiis et aequinoctiis*, lines 230-233, in B. Botte, *Les Origines de la Noël et de l'Epiphanie, étude historique*, Textes et études liturgiques, vol. 1 (Louvain: Abbaye du Mont César, 1932) 99.

19. So, e.g., Hansjörg Auf der Maur, *Feiern im Rhythmus der Zeit: Herrenfeste in Woche und Jahr*, vol. 5 of *Gottesdienst der Kirche: Handbuch der Liturgiewissenschaft* (Regensburg: Pustet, 1983) 167. For the dating of the mosaic, loc. cit., n. 68; also P. Jounel, *The Liturgy and Time*, vol. 4 of *The Church at Prayer* (Collegeville: The Liturgical Press, 1986) 78, n. 3.

20. Oscar Cullman, "The Origin of Christmas," *The Early Church* (Philadelphia: Westminster, 1956) 29-32. The view of Constantine presented in this frequently cited essay has now been seriously challenged by Robin Lane Fox, *Pagans and Christians* (New York: Viking, 1987).

21. Cf. Hans Lietzmann, *From Constantine to Julian*, vol. 3 of *A History of the Early Church* (New York: Scriber, 1950) 317; M.H. Shepherd, "The Liturgical Reform of Damasus I," in *Kyriakon. Festschrift Johannes Quasten*, vol. 2, (Münster/Westf.: Aschendorff, 1970) 854; Leonhard Fendt,

"Der heutige Stand der Forschung über das Geburtsfest Jesu am 25.XII und über Epiphanias," *Theologische Literaturzeitung* 78.1 (January 1953) cols. 1-10.

22. Thomas J. Talley, "Constantine and Christmas," *Gratias Agamus. Studia Liturgica* 17 (1987) 191-197. From his defeat of Licinius on 18 September 324 to his death in 337, Constantine was in Rome only from 18 July 326 to the end of September of that year, according to Gilbert Dagron, *Naissance d'une capitale: Constantinople et ses institutions de 330 à 451* (Paris: Presses Universitaires de France, 1974) 20, 33.

23. This is an anonymous gloss on a manuscript of a work by Dionysius bar Salibi who died in 1171. This manuscript was published by Assemani in *Bibliotheca Orientalis*, vol. 2 (Rome, 1721).

24. In addition to the data already adduced, cf. my *Origins of the Liturgical Year* 97-99. Cf. also F.C. Conybeare, "Ananias of Shirak upon Christmas," *The Expositor. Fifth Series* 4 (1896) 321-337. Ananias was an Armenian writer of the seventh century.

25. Roland Bainton, "Basilidian Chronology and New Testament Interpretation," *Journal of Biblical Literature* 42, parts I and II (1923). This research was later reissued as "The Origins of Epiphany," *Early and Medieval Christianity. The Collected Papers in Church History*, Series One (Boston, 1962) 22-38.

26. Twelve of the forty-nine days would fall in November (30-18=12), and thirty-one of the remaining thrity-seven in December; the remaining six days are in January.

27. Eduard Norden, *Die Geburt des Kindes: Geschichte einer religiosen Idee*, Studien der Bibliothek Warburg, vol. 3 (Leipzig and Berlin: B.G. Teubner, 1924) 38f. Norden first ascertained when the solstice would fall on 6 January, and then associated his hypothetical festival with Amenemhet I, whose reign at Thebes corresponded to that time. Recounting Norden's hypothesis, B. Botte (*Les Origines de la Noël et de l'Epiphanie* 71) spoke of "le calendrier d'Amenemhet I de Thèbes," and subsequent writers have spoken of the calendar of Amenemhet as if it were an item of documentary evidence. There is no such evidence.

28. Most recently in J.G. Davies, ed., *The New Westminster Dictionary of Liturgy and Worship* (Philadelphia: Westminster, 1986), s.v. "Christmas" 171.

29. Contemporary sources put both the feast of Dionysus on Andros and that of Aion at Alexandria on the nones (the 5th) of January.

30. W. Riedel and W.E. Crum, *The Canons of Athanasius of Alexandria*(London: Williams & Norgate, 1904) 26-27.

31. A.A. McArthur, *The Evolution of the Christian Year* (London: SCM, 1953) 69.

32. For the texts and documentation, cf. chapter 7 above.

33. In his response to the addresses at the Association of Diocesan Liturgy and Music Commissions Conference in Houston, Geoffrey Cuming took issue with this point, observing that Jesus periodically returns to Bethany in these chapters, thus marking them as more of a narrative than I have suggested. I respectfully remain unconvinced.

A Personal Afterword:
The Future of the Past

SOME YEARS AGO I WAS ASKED TO GIVE A LECTURE ON THE RELATION of tradition to the liturgical assembly in our day. I probably misunderstood the request, but I must confess that it struck me as weird. It was as if I had been asked to say a few words about the relation of water to fish. Still, I was aware that for some folk interested in liturgy today the significance of tradition is a secondary issue at best. I am not one of those folk, and I must confess that upon receiving that invitation my first arrogant impulse was to say, "*now* you ask me!" But that, I quickly realized, would be to assume a posture of innocence that would be not only self-serving, but dishonest. In fact, like too many of us, I have lived these recent decades with the conviction that my perception of the tradition should be immediately realized in liturgical reforms, even when I was unprepared to ask what I meant by "the tradition." Early on, of course, it was easier to speak of the tradition because I knew so miserably little that the little I did know all flowed together into one gloriously ecumenical vision that one could speak of as the undivided practice of the early church, a vision that in fact stemmed from the pitiful limitation of my information.

Limited information, however, was not the only source of the vision. Part of it was, in fact, a reaction to the tradition as it had been delivered to us, a reaction, that is to say, *against* the received tradition. During the latter days of World War II, I found myself in comfortable duty as an enlisted man at Fort Sill, Oklahoma, just a long block from the post chapel where, due to the extreme exigencies of wartime, there was celebrated (bizarre as it then seemed) a Roman Catholic Mass on weekday afternoons at the unheard of hour of 6:00P.M.. I would attend this Mass several afternoons a week, but these celebrations were painful to anyone who loved the liturgy. The Mass itself was completely inaudible, including the reading of the epistle and gospel. The priest would feed himself on the Latin text, which he whispered, while the rest of us recited aloud the rosary and the litany of Loretto, interrupted briefly for the institution narrative, or at least for a time of silence during which we were sure the priest was reciting the narrative, a supposition confirmed only by bells and elevations.

In those days, even an Episcopalian might believe that the great tradition of the Western Church to which we Anglo-Catholics so steadily appealed, had come upon sad days, that "the tradition" just had to mean something better than what recent history had in fact delivered. To one of my Mediterranean tastes, the rather dour chastity of the early communion on Sunday morning in the Episcopal church in nearby Lawton did not seem to be the true expression of the tradition so painfully caricatured by the "papistical sluttery" in which I wallowed on those weekday afternoons at the post chapel. The received liturgical tradition of the Episcopal Church was focused on the choral rendition of the morning office, and on most Sundays the only Mass was tucked away at that early morning hour as a concession to the piety of odd individuals. If for no other reason than that, the Episcopal Church seemed to represent but the other horn of a dilemma before which one could only dream of the tradition, not point to it.

Though it would be a few years before Gregory Dix would introduce me to the fact, the dream was already receiving some precision, if not substance, from the growing community of liturgical scholars, and I can remember well the excitement I shared in my last year at Sewanee with my new friend, a freshman named Joe Kavanagh (he would, of course, take another name at his monastic profession after his "submission to the Holy See," as the phrase went in those days), when month by month we would pour over *Orate Fratres*, marvelling at the prophetic boldness of H.A. Reinhold, stunned by the freshness of the vision of the Mystical Body that slowly took shape in our blossoming heads, and awed by the emergence of the authentic tradition out of the past, and, as it seemed, from between the horns of our Anglo-Catholic dilemma. Not from the sixteenth century would we take our identity, nor yet from the thirteenth, but from the re-emerging shape of the liturgy (to coin a phrase) of the undivided church of the first half of the first millennium. There, in the cool classicism of patristic liturgy—the bishop surrounded by the presbyteral college facing the people as they filed forward to deposit their gifts of bread and wine on a simple table that defined the center of the assembly over which the bishop presided in giving thanks—was the setting from which would flow into our distorted present the authentic tradition of the ancient undivided church.

And we really believed that! We believed it in spite of the fact that we knew perfectly well that whatever you want to say of the church of the first five centuries, you could never say that it was undivided; and, probably, more than would admit to it knew as well that there was no evidence whatsoever for a universal practice of celebration *versus populum* in the third, fourth, fifth, sixth, or seventh centuries. Unless his Notre Dame lectures were significantly revised for publication,[1] Jungmann was warning us as early as 1949 that the claim of historical precedent for celebration *versus populum* was often highly exaggerated, and that the question really came down to whether the altar stood in the west end of the nave or the east. Otto Nussbaum spent two hard-fought volumes seeking to marshall the archaeological evidence for Mass facing the people and failed to make a case, although the introduction to his work affords us a valuable documentation of the growth of this misconception during the nineteenth and early twentieth centuries.[2] It is a source of some relief to this liturgiologist, at least, that responsible authorities in Rome based the reform calling for Mass *versus populum* on something other than a historical foundation.[3] In fact, such an arrangement is profoundly Roman, since Roman churches from S. Cecelia in Trastevere to the Lateran basilica have a way of putting their altars toward the west end, with the result that the priest, following the widespread ancient custom of praying toward the east, would find himself facing the nave. In other situations, while the bishop might find himself presiding at the liturgy of the word facing the congregation from a cathedra in a *synthronon* in the east apse (or facing east with the people from a *bema* in the center of the nave), he would stand at the altar for the eucharistic prayer with his back to the people, not because he saw himself as a shepherd leading the flock, or as a practitioner of arcane arts that were none of their business, but just because he wanted to pray toward the east as did the people. This orientation in prayer was practiced by the Essenes at Qumran and was urged by early writers on prayer such as Tertullian and Origen. Hippolytus saw the church as a ship whose prow is in the east.[4]

In a religious culture from which such concern for orientation in prayer has vanished, there is no way that one can assess the relation of contemporary arrangement of the assembly to moments of history dominated by that concern. What is noteworthy in all this is not so much that our liturgical assembly does or does not reflect the shape of such assemblies in other times and places, but that for so long our concern for a more interpersonal climate in worship managed to convince us that such a shape of the assembly was, indeed, profoundly traditional. This shows the power of "tradition" as a metaphor, but it also reveals the way in which our present dissatisfaction and our hope for a better tomorrow works to filter the data we admit and therefore shapes our perception of the amorphous "early church," a perception which we see as the true locus of the tradition. When reformation is the agenda, hope dictates memory and the future tends to shape the past.

This, however, works both ways. It is not only novelty that is defended by appeal to the past, but also presuppositions too deeply entrenched to accept reformation. The defense of such primary concerns in a time of reform will lead to new novelties for which the authority of tradition is claimed. We have seen this in the preoccupation with the institution narrative in reform of the eucharistic prayers.

In the Western Churches the institution narrative has held a central place in relation to the theology of eucharistic consecration. One may doubt that either Ambrose or Chrysostom was concerned to pinpoint a "moment of consecration," but both spoke highly of the relevance of the institution narrative to our theology of eucharistic consecration. Yet such has been the ecumenical dynamic of recent liturgical reform that it has seemed well to lay the ghost of controversy regarding the importance of the invocation of the Holy Spirit in that regard by including such an invocation in all new eucharistic prayers. In many quarters, including the Roman Catholic Church and the Church of England, this was accomplished in what some believed to be a graceful and irenic manner by the simple expedient of situating the invocation of the Spirit for the consecration of the gifts prior to the institution narrative. At the same time, the structure of those prayers that had of old been characterized by such an invocation after the institution narrative, whether that of the *Apostolic Tradition* or the Alexandrian Basil or whatever, was also honored by the insertion of a further invocation of the Spirit upon the communicants following the narrative and anamnesis. Having discussed above the theological implications of such an anaphoral structure, this is not the place to contest either the grace or the irenic force of such a solution. It is sufficient to say that both the Congregation for Divine Worship (when confirmed by the pope) and the General Synod of the Church of England are competent bodies for the promulgation of liturgical forms.

What must be contested is whether this solution reflects, as we are frequently told, an ancient Alexandrian tradition. This is not a matter of eucharistic theology, but simply of clear reading of the documents of the Alexandrian eucharistic liturgy. None of them displays such a division of the concerns for which the Spirit is invoked. As argued above, all but one of our Egyptian sources invoke the Spirit for the consecration of the gifts only after they have been offered in anamnesis of Christ's death and resurrection,[5] and this one exception (a fragment from Dêr Balyzeh in Upper Egypt from the sixth or seventh century, and therefore roughly contemporary with the Gregorian recension of the Canon Missae) is so fragmentary that it is quite impossible to assess the relationship of this invocation to other sensitive aspects of anaphoral structure. Unlike Sarapion or St. Mark, Dêr Balyzeh, does, in fact, display a fully articulated epiklesis for the transformation of the gifts prior to the institution narrative. And if this is the sole question we wish to ask, then we are likely to be satisfied with such skimpy evidence as this fragment affords. In such a case, we will fail to notice that the anamnesis following that epiklesis and the institution narrative makes no oblation of those putatively consecrated gifts, and we will, it seems, fail to ask whether there was any oblation at all and, if so, whether it fell prior to the *Sanctus* as in St. Mark. In other words, the much-cited ancient Alexandrian tradition for a double epiklesis is simply a function of our limited inquiry. We have asked only if there has ever been an epiklesis prior to the institution narrative, and we have asked the question in only that form because we had our answer already to the question we therefore did not ask, namely, what is the role of the institution narrative in the eucharistic prayer?

In like manner, as regards the shape of the assembly, we asked only whether in the early church the celebrant prayed the anaphora facing the people, and for this limited form of the question the evidence of the Roman basilicas with their sheer drop in front of the altar was sufficient. Of course he did. But because we did not ask why such was true at Rome and not true at Paris or Constantinople, we were able to leap to the conclusion that it was once true everywhere, and begin to build on this supposed fact an ecclesiology and a liturgical spirituality reflective less of our past than of our present. And this is just fine, but the resulting arrangements, whether of the assembly or the eucharistic prayer, are "traditional" only in the sense that this kind of historical hanky-panky has been going on for a long time.

Now this is not to say that the appeal to the tradition is simply a pack of lies. It is to say, on the other hand, that when the tradition as we have received it fails to satisfy our present needs, then we begin to look at the past through future-colored glasses. This is a pious approach to the future, but it is a hampered, if not knuckle-headed, approach to the past. The past must be courted with less urgency than that customarily felt by those engaged in planning next Sunday's liturgy.

This is the beauty of the Rite for the Christian Initiation of Adults. There is presently very little need for it. The tradition of infant baptism is strong among us, and is alive and well. This fact is beginning to enjoy some serious assessment in terms of its ultimate appropriateness for the life of the church in our own time, and the assessment is not carried on in a liturgical vacuum.

The Rite for the Christian Initiation of Adults provides a context for such discussion, but it was formulated out of a patient and relatively disinterested study of the past, and free from the complex pressures that would have come into play if it had been intended to displace infant baptism in a radical reform.

We are beginning to see exciting experiments with a restored catechumenate and the rites for such a process are, I believe, a model of contemporary adaptation of patristic practice. But I doubt that this could have been so had these rites been expected to have a radical and immediate impact on pastoral praxis. The demands of such praxis too often run counter to the ascesis of the historian.

Liturgists, however, find themselves on both sides of the fence, and this presents problems. On the one hand, we are expected to be those experts who know more than anybody about how to organize the worship of the assembly, and, on the other hand, we are supposed to know all this against the background of a meticulous examination of the past practice of the church, an examination boiled down to a distillate that we call "the tradition." To one extent or another, the outcome is supposed to represent the contemporary realization of that tradition. Does it do so? Does the present stage of our cultic evolution stand in continuity with the liturgical life of the past? Or have we reformed ourselves into a new beginning which will have to grow itself into a fresh moment of tradition? Well, these questions are badly put, and therefore the answer to all of them is both yes and no.

Of course, our liturgy is in continuity with our past, and that is true of some of its more novel features. The assembly worships God in its own vernacular language, and such is certainly highly traditional. This is why Rome's Greek liturgy became Latin. But if our liturgy ever becomes at all stable, then we must expect that the development of language is going to continue to a point that will leave even the rather plain expressions of the ICEL translations sounding hieratic—though this will take some time! The contrast between Church Slavonic and the Russian of the United Nations is not all that different from the contrast between our current English and that of the King James Bible or the *Book of Common Prayer* or Shakespeare. If Elizabethan language now sounds hieratic, this did not prevent Shakespeare from telling bawdy jokes in just that language. Indeed, one might argue that the evolution of the English language to a point that would leave Elizabethan English sounding hieratic was a significant factor in evoking a new and more mystically oriented spirituality in England in the nineteenth century.[6] Thoroughly intelligible religious language is a chimera, if not a contradiction in terms. I have been amused to note that the rendering of the American *Book of Common Prayer* into contemporary English has been accompanied by a fresh proliferation of cultic words borrowed from Hebrew and Greek. *Hosanna, Alleluia, Kyrie eleison* and the like are much more common in our liturgy today than they were in earlier Prayer Books.

For all that, our liturgies today are thoroughly contemporary, and this also is highly traditional. The liturgy at our parish churches on Sunday will be no more contemporary than was that at the old Hagia Sophia in the days of Chrysostom. In a very real sense, all liturgy is always contemporary and cannot be otherwise. The language, even if Latin, is always spoken with the accents of the contemporary vernacular of the one speaking. Elizabethan English spoken with a Texas drawl does not take one away from Texas, nor does a Gothic or Georgian church building equipped with air conditioning ducts. The question is not whether a liturgy is traditional or contemporary, but rather how much of our history we are prepared to carry along with us. And for our own generation, the answer seems to be: very little, but all that is needed.

And this seems a valid claim. Having unpacked a very great deal of no longer visibly useful obfuscation, there can be little doubt that the reformed liturgy of our own day manifests those broad lines of the liturgical tradition that are constant in all rites in all ages, and this not only preserves our sense of continuity with every part of our past, but more importantly it has revealed a community with churches from which we have been separated and has invited us to contemplate a unity in Christ with which our several polities must sooner or later come to grips.

There is another sense, however, in which our assembly today is not traditional and will have trouble becoming traditional, and I almost hesitate to speak of it. One of the profound characteristics of any traditional cultic life is its ritual quality. A ritual, as anthropologists and historians of religion have repeatedly pointed out, is not planned; it is given. It is not something we devise, but that to which we give ourselves. And it is difficult to see the western eucharist in these terms today. Indeed, the ritual quality of an assembly seems to be almost inversely related to the liturgical sophistication of its participants, and especially of its president. I do not mean that it is not serious. There are, of course, silly liturgies still, and they must be condemned strenuously and consistently until they disappear. But this is not the problem. Those of us who are deeply involved in historical, theological, and pastoral consideration of the liturgy are, by this very fact, virtually incapable of leaving it alone. Loving it, we fondle it until it is misshapen. Certain that with a bit more planning it can be somehow "better" next Sunday than last, we deny the assembly one thing that it desperately needs: immersion in a ritual pattern whose authority, dimly understood but powerfully experienced, transcends our own ingenuity, erudition, and energy. At the risk of being hoist on my own petard, I must confess that we need the insight and the faith to obey the rubrics. It is a sign of our malaise that it seems shocking today to hear a liturgist say a thing like this.

Some headway is being made, I believe, in this matter. At least within my hearing, it seems, people have stopped trying to "create rituals." I think we have backed off from such nonsense. *Hair* had a ritual quality, as did *Equus*, and they may indeed have functioned ritually for the actors. Those of us in the audience, however, may have been deeply touched by the archaic quality of these productions, but we were not fed by it all the days of our lives.

The ritual quality once possessed by western liturgy has been modulated at the very least, and will almost surely never be as it was again. The days are simply gone when a glimpse at the ordo in the sacristy and the flipping of a few ribbons would deliver not only all the texts to be used but the musical settings of most of them. A new freedom has entered into the rubric itself, and there are decisions to be made, options to be chosen among, hymns to be selected, intercessions to be framed, etc., etc., etc. And this degree of freedom seems to be not only good and desirable, but very nearly inexorable.

Given this prescription of freedom, we need to examine the spirit in which we exercise it, and a part of this may well call us to relinquish some part of our hard-won ingenuity and the presupposition that our critical acumen is supposed to reshape some little aspect of the liturgy every time we read another journal article. As beautiful, as meaningful, and as impressive as our liturgical designs are, they need a deeper authority than our own. And such authority simply appears in the celebration when we accede to it. It is not precisely in the ritual phenomena, but in the souls of the one who presides over it and those who participate in it. It is an authority won by obedience. It is, indeed, the authority of obedience.

I had an experience of this some months ago. Having worked one Sunday morning until it was too late to make it to a convenient 9:00 Mass, then 10:00 at the nearby parish church, and finally the 11:00 at a parish a bit farther away, I realized that I was teetering on the brink of damnation, and tore myself away from whatever it was I was fiddling with and got dressed just in time to be only two minutes late for the last Mass at 1:00 at Holy Guardian Angels, the Roman Catholic parish across Tenth Avenue from the seminary. It is a pleasant building, perhaps a bit too self-consciously Italian to be considered an architectural monument, but a lovely church nonetheless. By that hour, of course, the pastor had completed his duties for the morning, and the priest at this Mass was a youngster, only shortly out of seminary, I would assume. Nothing in his manner suggested that he was a liturgy buff, and the mysteries unfolded just like the missalette said they would. I watched with interest since I was utterly convinced, and still am, that I was seeing here not the work of some highly honed mystagogue, but simply the result of a standard theological education on a young man who had always wanted to be a priest and still did, one who knew no more about the liturgy than Dunwoodie required of him, and who had been carefully trained in accordance with the Missal of Paul VI. The total experience, I must say, was profoundly encouraging, partly because this was one of the few churches in Manhattan that required no serious renovation after the council, having a marble table altar standing free under a handsome baldachino. The young priest standing there seemed to have been standing there always (the altar is in the west end of this tiny basilica) and evoked memories of tenth-century ivories of liturgical scenes. I noticed that, having filled the chalice, he added some water to it. He may have believed this was surely done at the Last Supper, or he may have known that it was so in the time of Justin Martyr, and he may even have been aware of the rather constant tradition of symbolic interpretation that this action has enjoyed since the time of Cyprian. He may, indeed, have found it meaningful. But I had the distinct impression that he did it because he was a priest performing a ritual, and this was what the ritual required him to do. Having shown the bread and the cup to the people during the canon, he actually genuflected on each occasion. And having broken the host at the fraction, he broke off another small fragment and placed it in the chalice. Was he thinking of the *fermentum* of which Innocent wrote to Decentius, or the *sancta* ceremony in Ordo I? Had he read Andrieu's *Immixtio et Consecratio*? I somehow had the impression that the answer to all these questions was no, and that it didn't make any difference. And for this reason, I felt deeply the strength of the tradition in that assembly of people who were strangers to me. This liturgy was what the reform had produced, and it was clear, strong, direct, and profoundly archaic. That is to say, as with all good ritual, it was powerfully authoritative. I could see no way in which the election or appointment of a new liturgy committee could alter that authority, for it was not made on the premises. While there may well have been older layfolk there for whom this liturgy was still new, for me it was as old as the history of our people, and as fresh as it has ever been in those twenty centuries.

Now, I don't want to be a wet blanket or a spoilsport, but I simply do not have the sensitivity or the ingenuity or the erudition to generate this sense of authority. And neither, I am sure, did that kid. Such authority resides in the ritual itself, and our best intentioned and best informed attempts to improve upon it had better be good, because the power they dissipate is great. I am not concerned with law, and I hope none of us is. But I am concerned with ritual as a given to which I conform myself. And I guess I hope that—to one degree or another—we all are.

Given the flexibility built into our liturgies today, this ritual sense can never become a straightjacket. But forgetfulness of it can reduce our liturgies to mere performances. The reformation is not over, and by God's grace it never will be, but we should not suppose that everything is still up for grabs the way it was or seemed to be in the years just following the council. I see no reason at all why *Liturgiewissenschaft* should have an immediately practical goal, any more than classical studies should. But, like biblical studies, liturgical studies will continue to have a powerful critical role to play. As I have already confessed, I am deeply disappointed with the present form of the eucharistic prayers in the Roman Missal, and I trust that we shall see further movement in that matter sooner or later—probably later. But for now, it is a battle to be fought in the journals, not at the altar.

Our past can still shape our future, and if God gives us strength to grind our books, it will. The tradition we study has never been one fixed pattern, and never can be, for it is an inherently dynamic concept. To this extent, acceptance of the tradition is the acceptance of a history of change. But movements of reform have a way of rejecting the past, risking new patterns of disunity. Renewal itself will be better served as we seek, observe, and honor the continuities that connect us with all of Christian history and with all who honor it today. Such must be the work of many disciplines, but my own hope is that by patient study of the historical development of liturgical life and by careful promulgation of our findings, we may all be moved, actually edged, toward deeper realization of the unity of our God in the one Body of Jesus Christ, the same yesterday and today and forever.

Notes

1. J. Jungmann, *The Early Liturgy to the Time of Gregory the Great*(Notre Dame: University of Notre Dame Press, 1959) 137-138.

2. O. Nussbaum, *Der Standort des Liturgen am christlichen Altar vor dem Jahre 1000: Eine archeologische und liturgiegeschichtliche Untersuchung*, Theophaneia, vol. 18 (Bonn: Peter Hanstein Verlag, 1965) 17-20.

3. Ferdinando Dell' Oro, commenting on this provision of the instruction, presented it as intended to facilitate the active participation of the faithful, and added: "For this reason also, the traditional and characteristic position of Christian prayer toward the east is to be abandoned..." In William Barauna and Jovian Lang, eds., *The Liturgy of Vatican II*, vol. 2 (Chicago: Franciscan Herald Press, 1966) 320f.

4. *On Christ and Antichrist* 59 (Ante-Nicene Fathers, vol. 5, 216).

5. The Louvain papyrus fragment (reportedly confirmed by an un-published Greek text at Barcelona) presents both the anamnesis-obla-tion and the consecratory invocation, in this order, before the institution narrative.

6. This hypothesis was framed, as far as I am aware, by one of my classmates in the seminary, Fr. Henry Breul, now Rector of St. Thomas' Church, Washington, D.C.